Delicious Meals
MADE EASY

120 Time-Saving PRESSURE COOKER RECIPES

PARTNERS IN
PUBLISHING

Published by Partners In Publishing, Natick, Massachusetts

First Printing in January 2016

Authors: Bob Warden and Mona Dolgov

The Partners in Publishing Culinary Team

Editors: Cali Rich and Lynn Clark

Book Design: Leslie Anne Feagley

Food Photography: Gary Sloan

Creative Director, Photography: Anne Welch

Recipe Concepts: Christian Stella

Recipe Testing and Development: The Partners in Publishing Culinary Team

Library of Congress Cataloging-in-Publication Data has been applied for.

Second Edition

ISBN 978-1-4951-8373-7

52495

10   9   8   7   6   5   4

Printed in Canada

TABLE OF CONTENTS

Pressure Cooking Made Simple

The *Delicious Meals Made Easy* cookbook was developed with you in mind! Each recipe is simple to make, uses readily available ingredients, and tastes delicious. It includes a complete breadth of recipes, from appetizers to easy weekday favorites, comfort classics, healthier recipes, and decadent desserts. We also wanted to make sure that when you make the recipes, they actually turn out like the photos in the book. After all, you really do first eat with your eyes! There is nothing worse than being hooked by a beautiful photo, taking the time to shop for and prepare the ingredients, and painstakingly following the recipe, only to have the finished dish look nothing like you expected! Every photograph in this book illustrates food taken directly from the pressure cooker. We wanted every recipe photo to be a WOW, and empower you to give it a try.

The healthier recipes in the book, labeled "Our Healthy Take", have lower-fat meats, lots of vegetables and beans, and minimal oils and fats. The pressure cooker is an ideal appliance for vegetables, healthy soups and stews, and whole grains like rice and quinoa. Marinades can also infuse into the leaner meats, helping to maintain their juiciness. Yes, you now can have wonderfully delicious meals, and they can actually be better for you, too!

And, because it's nearly impossible to find reduced-sodium, gluten-free, USDA-approved beef, chicken, and vegetable stocks with high-quality flavor, we teamed up with Great Flavors® to create a complete line of squeezable, healthier stock concentrates. Now you can make better-tasting and more affordable instant stocks for your pressure-cooked recipes.

Pressure Cooker 101

The power of pressure cooking is truly magical. It's amazing that a delicious meal can be cooked in one third of the time required by a typical home oven. How does it do that? It is made possible by the laws of thermal dynamics. Steam is a far more efficient medium to transfer heat than air or even boiling water, and therefore it can heat food faster. In addition, when steam is put under pressure in a modern pressure cooker, the cooker is able to safely maintain a pressurized and saturated steam environment that will constantly transfer heat three times faster than a dry 350-degree oven.

By cooking with steam, you retain all the moisture of your food, so that the moist and juicy textures are maintained. For example, a five-pound roast in a dry conventional home oven can lose up to 40% percent of its weight through evaporation. In a pressure cooker, 99 percent of the moisture remains either in the roast, or in the cooking liquid, to produce a tasty sauce or gravy. The roast retains the moisture in the meat, which results in great texture, extra juiciness, and more intense flavor. In a pressure cooker, the fibrous connective tissue of even the toughest cut of meat will melt in your mouth. The meat can never be dried out, because it is impossible for it to become dry in a steam environment. In restaurants, cheaper, tougher cuts of meats are traditionally cooked in a pressure cooker, and magically become restaurant quality.

Pressure Cooking— Time and Energy Saver

The pressure cooker is also a true time-saver for meal preparation, and will soon become your favorite kitchen appliance. You can get dinner on the table in next to no time. Braises, such as pot roast, pulled pork, chicken, short ribs, and lamb shanks, become fork tender in 45 to 90 minutes, compared to an oven braise, taking from three to

five hours. Short ribs are one of the best entrees served by top restaurant chefs and are typically cooked slowly for eight to ten hours. Now that pressure cookers are becoming popular again, you can get the same result at home in only 90 minutes! See our Hungarian Braised Short Ribs on page 87.

In addition, the pressure cooker is much more energy efficient that a large oven, because it cooks faster and uses much less energy while it is cooking. It also doesn't heat up your kitchen, which a great advantage during summer months and in warm climates.

Today's electric pressure cookers are very safe and easy to use as well. You do not have to try to guess when optimal pressure is reached, and you do not need to make any stovetop adjustments during the entire cooking process. And the pressure cooker will even keep your meal warm when you are done.

In addition, you can brown and sauté meats and vegetables together right in the same pot, prior to pressure cooking. The pressure cooker can also function as a saucepan later, allowing you to prepare gravies from the delicious meat and vegetable juices that have been produced. That's right! You don't have to dirty separate skillets or saucepans on the stovetop. One pot does it all.

Converting Pressure Cooker Recipes to Slow Cooker Recipes

Most electric pressure cookers, including the Elite 8-quart, have a slow cooker setting. Sometimes you will prefer to have a meal waiting for you when you come home after a long day at work, and even a fast pressure cooker may not be fast enough! But in just minutes, you can prepare your meal in advance. It is very easy to convert one-pot, complete-meal recipes from pressure cooking to slow cooking. For most recipes, you will simply use the same preparation steps, up to the cooking process. You will then set the slow cooker time for somewhere between a minimum of four hours (for such foods as pre-soaked beans, braises, lean meats, and pre-cooked ground beef dishes) and a maximum of eight hours (for tougher meat cuts and dry beans). The flexible modern pressure cooker can do it all!

Better-For-You Pressure Cooking

Pressure cookers provide so many advantages in cooking, both from a nutritional and a flavor perspective. You can cook fresh vegetables, beans and lean meats in a shorter period of time, using less water. This essentially means that more nutrients remain in the foods. For

example, you can make an incredible, flavor-packed Lentil Soup (page 36) in less than an hour! Or a tender, nutty Brown Rice Pilaf (page 132) in less than 30 minutes—a savings of half the time! Studies have shown that pressure cooking reduces the phytic acid content of grains and legumes, which increases the nutrient availability and makes them more digestible.* Pressure cooking may simply be the healthiest way of all to cook your beans and grains.

Pressure cooking seafood and lean meats is a quick and easy way to keep them moist and to infuse them with flavor. Salmon filets are perfectly cooked every time in just 5 minutes! There are several boneless chicken breast recipes in this book, made with mouthwatering marinades that infuse flavors during the cooking process. Check out the unique ingredient combinations in the Honey Lime Chicken (page 53), the Take out Thai Chicken (page 49), and the Amazing Apricot Chicken (page 59). The Amazing Apricot Chicken, for example, combines boneless, skinless chicken breasts with tart apricots, garlic, lemon, and soy sauce. The result? Juicy, healthy, tasty and delicious!

Throughout the book, you will see some recipes with a symbol called Healthy Take. These recipes are selected because of their better-for-you ingredients. Many of them use extra-lean meats, but thanks to the power of the pressure cooker, the meat is robustly seasoned without the need for added fat. Eating healthier with enhanced flavor is surely a win-win situation!

We've included charts in the back of the book with cooking times for a variety of lean meats, legumes, grains, and vegetables. Use this guide as a fun and creative way to put your own spin on your next pressure-cooked meal!

Pressure Cooker Fundamentals

It is highly recommended that you read your cooker's manual from front to back to fully understand how to safely and correctly operate your specific pressure cooker. Be particularly mindful of pressure output, pressure release, and overall pressure cooker size. Note that these recipes were created using an Elite 8 quart pressure cooker, that uses 12 PSI.

Releasing the Pressure: Quick vs. Natural Release

There are two methods used to release the pressure of a pressure cooker and this book uses both, depending on the needs of the

*Source: http://link.springer.com/article/10.1007%2FBF01088088?LI=true#page-1

recipe involved. "A quick release" typically involves opening a steam valve to let the pressure escape all at once, while a "natural release" takes approximately 15-30 minutes, to allow the pressure to escape naturally. We've typically added 20 minutes to the "cook time" for these recipes to allow for the steam release. For detailed information on how to perform a quick release with your pressure cooker, consult its manual. We do highly recommend using an oven mitt when quick releasing in order to protect your hands from the hot steam.

How to Adjust Recipes if Your Pressure Cooker Has a Different Volume

Unfortunately, there is no direct ratio between the volumes of food for large vs. smaller pressure cookers. We have created a chart on page 197 to help you make the appropriate adjustments for the recipes in this book.

About Cooking Times

The cooking times at the top of each recipe in this book refer to the amount of time the food is actually cooked under pressure. Time is also added for natural release if applicable. These times do not include the time it takes for your particular pressure cooker to come up to pressure. Electronic pressure cookers automatically start the countdown once the desired pressure is reached. Assume that all recipes will take an additional 5 to 15 minutes to come up to pressure. Also, as already noted, natural-release recipes require 15 to 30 minutes to release pressure.

Cooking from Frozen

One of the biggest advantages of pressure cooking is that you can cook pasta and small cuts of meat directly out of the freezer, with no thawing necessary! Although we did develop our recipes using fresh or thawed meat (unless otherwise noted), we have added a column for optional frozen cooking times in the meat cooking time charts. Note that the additional time should be added to the closed pressure cooking process. Also, keep in mind that frozen cuts can not be browned. Instead, add 1 additional teaspoon of the appropriate flavor of Great Flavors® Stock Concentrates before pressure cooking. Because Great Flavors® concentrates do contain some salt, you may want to reduce the salt called for in the recipe, if desired.

Home Canning Basics

There are two methods used in home canning: the water bath (boiling water covering jars) method and the pressure canning method. Both can be done in the electric pressure cooker.

The Water Bath Method

This is a simple way to get started if you are a beginner; the water-bath method is perfect for canning high acid fruits, such as tomatoes, berries, or pickles, which do not require a long processing time under pressure. The vacuum-sealed acidic environment is enough to keep foods safe and delicious in your pantry.

Filled glass canning jars are placed on the rack that comes with your pressure cooker, and processed covered in boiling water for the time specified in the recipe. After this process, the jars are removed and left to cool; the lids automatically seal shut and a vacuum is created. Simply screw on jar rings, and your canned foods are ready for storage in your pantry .

The Pressure Canning Method

Pressure canning, as the name implies, is done "under pressure" in your electric pressure cooker. Jars are placed on the canning rack and only partially submerged, so they can be processed at the higher temperature of the pressure cooker. Simply follow the instructions for each recipe, using this method.

Pressure canning may seem intimidating for beginners, but it is really very easy. In this cookbook, we have selected simple recipes using both methods in order to get you started. Canning is perfect for making fresh fruit jams, sauces, salsas, pie fillings, relishes and more! It's a great way to take advantage of fresh fruits and vegetables in season, and enjoy them year round.

APPETIZERS

Hawaiian Cocktail Meatballs, 19

Eggplant Red Pepper Caponata

Serves:
10 to 12

Prep Time:
15 minutes

Pressure Cooking Time:
7 minutes

Release Method:
QUICK

Classic Italian restaurants often serve caponata with bread sticks as an appetizer. Now you make this simple recipe and keep it on hand. You can freeze it and even can it using the pressure cooker, as you would a tomato sauce.

Ingredients:

2 tablespoons vegetable oil

1 pound eggplant, cut into 1-inch cubes

2 medium onions, thinly sliced

5 cloves garlic, minced

2 red bell peppers, seeded and chopped

1 (14.5 oz.) can diced tomatoes

3 tablespoons lemon juice

1 teaspoon sugar

¾ teaspoon curry powder

Salt and pepper

1 tablespoon minced fresh cilantro

Directions:

1. Add all ingredients except cilantro to inner pot. Close and lock lid. Adjust pressure valve on top to AIRTIGHT, set COOKING TIME to 7 minutes, and press START.

2. When cooking cycle has finished, release pressure by carefully setting valve to EXHAUST on top of lid. Once all of pressure has released, turn lid, unlock, and open.

3. Drain cooking liquid, and transfer to serving dish. Add cilantro, stir to combine ingredients.

TIP Serve with your favorite cracker, toasted pita, or for an easy and elegant appetizer, spread goat cheese on toasted baguette and top with caponata.

Buffalo Wings

Quick and easy pressure-cooked wings are a much healthier alternative to fried. These hot and tasty wings are ready in just half an hour, and make instant party food.

Serves:
8 to 10

Prep Time:
15 minutes

Pressure Cooking Time:
15 minutes

Release Method:
QUICK

Ingredients:

2 tablespoons vegetable oil

4 pounds chicken wings, drum and wings separated

1 (12 oz.) bottle buffalo wing sauce

¼ cup water

3 tablespoons unsalted butter

2 cups blue cheese dressing

Celery sticks

Directions:

1. Add oil to inner pot. Set COOKING TIME to 15 minutes and press START. Heat oil about 5 minutes. Add wings and cook until browned, about 10 minutes. Press CANCEL.

2. Add wing sauce, water, and butter. Close and lock lid. Adjust pressure valve on top to AIRTIGHT, set COOKING TIME to 15 minutes, and press START.

3. When cooking cycle has finished, release pressure by carefully setting valve to EXHAUST on top of lid. Once all of pressure has released, turn lid, unlock, and open.

4. Toss wings to completely coat with sauce. Transfer to a serving dish and serve with blue cheese dressing and celery sticks.

TIP To make sweet chili wings instead, substitute 1 (15 oz.) bottle Thai sweet chili sauce for the buffalo sauce and eliminate the blue cheese dressing and celery sticks.

Hawaiian Cocktail Meatballs

This quick and easy pressure cooker recipe is infused with the pineapple and ginger flavors of your favorite Asian restaurant. It will become your favorite recipe to bring to a party.

Serves:
8 to 10

Prep Time:
10 minutes

Pressure Cooking Time:
15 minutes

Release Method:
QUICK

Ingredients:

2 pounds frozen cocktail meatballs

3 cups fresh pineapple chunks

2 green bell peppers, seeded and chopped

¼ cup rice vinegar

¼ cup light brown sugar

2 tablespoons low-sodium soy sauce

1 tablespoon minced fresh ginger

1 tablespoon toasted sesame seeds

Directions:

1. Add all ingredients to inner pot. Close and lock lid. Adjust pressure valve on top to AIRTIGHT, set COOKING TIME to 15 minutes, and press START.

2. When cooking cycle has finished, release pressure by carefully setting valve to EXHAUST on top of lid. Once all of pressure has released, turn lid, unlock, and open.

3. Stir to combine ingredients.

TIP **This recipe can be easily doubled to serve a large group. For a party, set the pressure cooker to WARM when the meatballs are done and they will be ready when your guests arrive.**

Barbecue Brisket Mini Sliders

Brisket is perfect for the slow cooker. This tough cut of meat gets super tender after cooking and soaks up all the flavors of the BBQ sauce. The bright and creamy recipe for coleslaw complements the rich BBQ flavor.

Serves:
10 to 12

Prep Time:
15 minutes

Pressure Cooking Time:
1 hour, 20 minutes (includes pressure release time)

Release Method:
NATURAL

Ingredients:

3 pounds beef brisket, cut into 4-inch pieces

Salt and pepper

2 tablespoons vegetable oil

½ cup beef broth, we recommend Great Flavors® Beef Stock Concentrate

1 (18 oz.) bottle barbecue sauce

½ small head green cabbage, shredded

½ small head purple cabbage, shredded

1 medium carrot, peeled and grated

1 medium onion, grated

1 cup mayonnaise

3 tablespoons apple cider vinegar

12 slider buns (see tip)

Directions:

1. Season beef with salt and pepper. Add oil to inner pot. Set COOKING TIME to 15 minutes and press START. Heat oil about 5 minutes. Add beef to inner pot and cook until browned, about 10 minutes. Press CANCEL.

2. Add broth and barbecue sauce to inner pot. Close and lock lid. Adjust pressure valve on top to AIRTIGHT, set COOKING TIME to 1 hour, and press START.

3. When cooking cycle has finished, let pressure drop NATURALLY. Once all of pressure has released, turn lid, unlock, and open.

4. Transfer beef to a large bowl and shred with two forks. Add some cooking liquid back to shredded beef until moistened.

5. In a large bowl, combine both cabbages, carrot, onion, mayonnaise, and vinegar.

6. Serve brisket on slider buns topped with coleslaw.

TIP A heartier whole wheat or ciabatta slider bun will hold up better with the juicy barbecue beef and coleslaw.

Serves:
8

Prep Time:
20 minutes

**Pressure
Cooking Time:**
8 minutes

Release Method:
QUICK

 # Italian-Infused Artichokes

These delicious artichokes are ready in just 8 minutes instead of the typical 30 to 40 minutes it takes to cook them in a steamer. Adding the garlic and mayonnaise dip makes them special enough for a formal dinner.

Ingredients:

ARTICHOKES

8 medium artichokes

1 cup Italian dressing

½ cup water

Salt and pepper

SAUCE

1 cup mayonnaise

2 cloves garlic, minced

1 tablespoon grated lemon zest plus 3 tablespoons juice

Directions:

1. Remove tough outer leaves of artichokes until light yellow leaves. Cut off top ⅓ of artichoke. Trim end of stem and cut away tough outer layer.

2. Add artichokes, Italian dressing, and water to inner pot. Close and lock lid. Adjust pressure valve on top to AIRTIGHT, set COOKING TIME to 8 minutes, and press START.

3. When cooking cycle has finished, release pressure by carefully setting valve to EXHAUST on top of lid. Once all of pressure has released, turn lid, unlock, and open.

4. In a small bowl, combine mayonnaise, garlic, lemon zest, and juice. Serve sauce with artichokes.

TIP When you get to the center of the artichoke, use a spoon and scrape away the fuzzy, inedible choke.

Fresh Hummus

Once you try making this, you will never buy hummus again! Made from scratch with dried chickpeas, tahini, cumin, garlic and lemon, this creamy version is quick, easy, and delicious.

Serves:
10 to 12

Prep Time:
5 minutes

Pressure Cooking Time:
54 minutes (includes pressure release time)

Release Method:
NATURAL & QUICK

Ingredients:

3 cups dried chickpeas, rinsed and picked over

5 cups water

6 cloves garlic

1 bay leaf

¼ cup tahini

3 tablespoons lemon juice

½ teaspoon ground cumin

Salt and pepper

2 tablespoons extra-virgin olive oil

2 tablespoons minced fresh parsley

Directions:

1. Add chickpeas to inner pot and cover with water by 1 inch. Close and lock lid. Adjust pressure valve on top to AIRTIGHT, set COOKING TIME to 4 minutes, and press START. When cooking cycle has finished, let pressure drop NATURALLY. Once all of pressure has released, turn lid, unlock, and open. Drain chick peas and return to pot.

2. Add water, garlic, and bay leaf. Close and lock lid. Adjust pressure valve on top to AIRTIGHT, set COOKING TIME to 30 minutes, and press START.

3. When cooking cycle has finished, release pressure by carefully setting valve to EXHAUST on top of lid. Once all of pressure has released, turn lid, unlock, and open.

4. Drain chickpeas, reserving liquid. Remove bay leaf.

5. Transfer chickpeas to a food processor. Add tahini, lemon juice, and cumin. Season with salt and pepper. Puree to a creamy consistency adding some reserved cooking liquid as needed.

6. Place hummus in serving bowl and drizzle with oil and parsley.

TIP To add different flavors to the hummus, add roasted red pepper, olives, or jalapeno, seeded and chopped, to food processor in step 5.

Serves:
8 to 10

Prep Time:
10 minutes

Pressure Cooking Time:
6 minutes +
20-minute
cooling period

Release Method:
QUICK

 # Baba Ghanoush

This fresh and creamy dip is simple to make and will be the hit of any party. The tahini sesame paste gives this dip its depth, while lemon juice adds brightness. Serve with warm pita bread or fresh vegetables.

Ingredients:

2 pounds eggplant, peeled, and cut into 2-inch pieces

1 medium onion, diced

4 cloves garlic, chopped

¼ cup water

¼ cup tahini

3 tablespoons lemon juice

¾ teaspoon smoked paprika

3 tablespoons extra-virgin olive oil

Salt and pepper

Directions:

1. Add eggplant, onion, garlic, and water to inner pot. Close and lock lid. Adjust pressure valve on top to AIRTIGHT, set COOKING TIME to 6 minutes, and press START.

2. When cooking cycle has finished, release pressure by carefully setting valve to EXHAUST on top of lid. Once all of pressure has released, turn lid, unlock, and open.

3. Let eggplant mixture cool for 20 minutes. Transfer mixture to a food processor. Add tahini, lemon juice, paprika, and oil. Puree to creamy consistency. Season with salt and pepper.

4. Transfer mixture to airtight container and cool completely before serving.

TIP The best eggplants for Baba Ghanoush are smaller varieties, such as Italian or Japanese eggplant. They are less bitter and aren't likely to be as watery.

Spinach and Artichoke Dip

No appetizer table is complete without this amazing dip, a favorite at all our family gatherings. It is rich, cheesy and chock full of flavor.

Serves:
8 to 10

Prep Time:
15 minutes

Pressure Cooking Time:
8 minutes

Release Method:
QUICK

Ingredients:

1 tablespoon vegetable oil

1 medium onion, chopped

2 (14 oz.) cans artichoke hearts, drained and chopped

2 (8 oz.) packages cream cheese, softened

½ cup ranch dressing

¾ cup sour cream

1 pound frozen chopped spinach, thawed

4 cloves garlic, minced

1 cup grated Parmesan cheese

Salt and pepper

Directions:

1. Add oil to inner pot. Set COOKING TIME to 15 minutes and press START. Heat oil about 5 minutes. Add onions and cook until softened, about 10 minutes. Press CANCEL.

2. Add artichokes, cream cheese, ranch dressing, sour cream, spinach, and garlic. Season with salt and pepper. Stir to combine ingredients. Close and lock lid. Adjust pressure valve on top to AIRTIGHT, set COOKING TIME to 8 minutes, and press START.

3. When cooking cycle has finished, release pressure by carefully setting valve to EXHAUST on top of lid. Once all of pressure has released, turn lid, unlock, and open.

4. Add Parmesan to dip, and stir to combine.

TIP Fresh vegetables, thin toasted chips, or chunks of bread make the best dippers.

French Onion Dip

Serves:
10 to 12

Prep Time:
20 minutes

Pressure Cooking Time:
20 minutes

Release Method:
QUICK

This onion dip tastes so much better than the kind you buy at the grocery store. You will get rave reviews with this savory and délicieuse version made from chopped fresh onions and herbs.

Ingredients:

2 tablespoons vegetable oil

2 medium onions, chopped

¼ cup malt vinegar

2 (8 oz.) packages cream cheese, softened

½ cup sour cream

2 tablespoons Worcestershire sauce

Salt and pepper

Directions:

1. Add oil to inner pot. Set COOKING TIME to 20 minutes and press START. Heat oil about 5 minutes. Add onions and cook until browned, about 15 minutes. Press CANCEL.

2. Add vinegar, cream cheese, sour cream, and Worcestershire. Season with salt and pepper. Close and lock lid. Adjust pressure valve on top to AIRTIGHT, set COOKING TIME to 20 minutes, and press START.

3. When cooking cycle has finished, release pressure by carefully setting valve to EXHAUST on top of lid. Once all of pressure has released, turn lid, unlock, and open.

4. Stir to combine ingredients.

Nacho Cheese Dip

Not just a party dish! In only 15 minutes, this cheese dip is on the table when unexpected company drops by. Serve it with chips, and you have easy nachos!

Serves:
10 to 12

Prep Time:
5 minutes

Pressure Cooking Time:
10 minutes

Release Method:
QUICK

Ingredients:

2 (15 oz.) cans pinto beans, drained and rinsed

1 (8 oz.) package cream cheese, softened

1 (16 oz.) pasteurized cheese, such as Velveeta®

1 (16 oz.) jar chunky salsa

2 teaspoons chili powder

Directions:

1. Add all ingredients to inner pot and stir to combine. Close and lock lid. Adjust pressure valve on top to AIRTIGHT, set COOKING TIME to 10 minutes, and press START.

2. When cooking cycle has finished, release pressure by carefully setting valve to EXHAUST on top of lid. Once all of pressure has released, turn lid , unlock, and open.

3. Stir dip and transfer to serving dish.

TIP For a spicy kick, add 2 chopped jalapeño peppers or 1/2 teaspoon cayenne pepper.

Serves:
10 to 12

Prep Time:
15 minutes

Pressure Cooking Time:
15 minutes

Release Method:
QUICK

Black Bean Chili Dip

Always a hit on game day, this hearty dip will lift your spirits even if your team loses. Want a lower fat version? Simply serve this beefy dip without the cheese and sour cream.

Ingredients:

1 tablespoon vegetable oil

2 pounds 95% lean ground beef

1 medium onion, chopped

1 (16 oz.) jar mild chunky salsa

1 tablespoon chili powder

1 teaspoon ground cumin

1 (15 oz.) can black beans, drained and rinsed

2 cups shredded pepper jack cheese

3 tablespoons minced fresh cilantro

1 cup sour cream

Directions:

1. Add oil to inner pot. Set COOKING TIME to 15 minutes and press START. Heat oil about 5 minutes. Add beef and cook until browned, about 10 minutes. Press CANCEL.

2. Add onion, salsa, chili powder, cumin, and black beans and stir to combine. Close and lock lid. Adjust pressure valve on top to AIRTIGHT, set COOKING TIME to 15 minutes, and press START.

3. When cooking cycle has finished, release pressure by carefully setting valve to EXHAUST on top of lid. Once all of pressure has released, turn lid, unlock, and open.

4. Stir in cheese, cilantro, and sour cream.

TIP For a spicier dip, add 1 or 2 jalapeños, seeded and chopped, with the onion in Step 2.

STEWS & SOUPS

Chunky Minestrone Barley Soup, 45

Cuban Mango Black Bean Chili

If you love black beans and rice, you're going to love this Cuban recipe that combines the same unique sweet, tangy, and spicy flavors. Fresh mangos and a lively blend of herbs and spices kick it up a notch. For a lighter version, you can swap out the ground pork with ground turkey. Or, eliminate the meat altogether for a vegetarian meal!

Serves:
8 to 10

Prep Time:
Overnight soak time*
+ 15 minutes

Pressure Cooking Time:
20 minutes

Release Method:
QUICK

Ingredients:

1 pound dried black beans, rinsed

1 pound ground pork

Salt and pepper

1 tablespoon vegetable oil

1 medium onion, chopped

5 cups chicken broth, we recommend Great Flavors® Chicken Stock Concentrate

2 mangoes, peeled and chopped, divided

1 (14.5 oz.) can petite diced tomatoes

1 habanero pepper, seeded and diced

1 tablespoon ground cumin

1 teaspoon dried oregano

2 bay leaves

2 tomatoes, seeded and diced

2 tablespoons fresh lime juice

¼ cup chopped fresh cilantro

Directions:

1. In a large bowl, cover beans with at least 3 inches of water. Refrigerate and soak overnight. Drain and rinse soaked beans and set aside.

2. Season pork with salt and pepper. Add oil to inner pot. Set COOKING TIME to 15 minutes and press START. Heat oil about 5 minutes. Add pork and cook until browned, about 10 minutes. Press CANCEL.

3. Add black beans, onion, broth, half of mango, canned tomatoes, habanero, cumin, oregano, and bay leaves, and stir to combine. Close and lock lid. Adjust pressure valve on top to AIRTIGHT, set COOKING TIME to 20 minutes, and press START.

4. When cooking cycle has finished, release pressure by carefully setting valve to EXHAUST on top of lid. Once all of pressure has released, turn lid, unlock, and open.

5. Add fresh tomato, lime juice, cilantro and remaining mango. Stir to combine.

TIP *Instead of soaking beans overnight, add beans to the pressure cooker and cover with water by 1 inch. Pressure cook for 4 minutes and let the pressure drop naturally. Drain the beans and use in step 3 of the recipe.

Serves:
8

Prep Time:
Overnight
soak time*
+ 15 minutes

**Pressure
Cooking Time:**
20 minutes

Release Method:
QUICK

 # Hearty Bean Soup

This filling soup is the perfect recipe for a cold wintry day. Sautéing the veggies first gives the soup added depth of flavor. This hearty and healthy recipe keeps it simple by using a prepared mix of dried beans, available in almost all grocery stores.

Ingredients:

1 pound bean soup mix

1 tablespoon vegetable oil

2 stalks celery, chopped

1 medium onion, chopped

1 red bell pepper, seeded and chopped

4 cups vegetable broth, we recommend Great Flavors® Vegetable Stock Concentrate

1 (14.5 oz.) can diced tomatoes

3 cloves garlic, minced

3 tablespoons tomato paste

1 tablespoon Italian seasoning, we recommend Great Flavors® Italian Seasoning

Salt and pepper

Directions:

1. In a large bowl, cover beans with at least 3 inches of water. Refrigerate and soak overnight. Drain and rinse soaked beans and set aside.

2. Add oil to inner pot. Set COOKING TIME to 15 minutes and press START. Heat oil about 5 minutes. Add celery, onion, and red pepper and cook until softened, about 10 minutes. Press CANCEL.

3. Add soaked beans, broth, diced tomatoes, garlic, tomato paste, and Italian seasoning. Season with salt and pepper and stir to combine.

4. Close and lock lid. Adjust pressure valve on top to AIRTIGHT, set COOKING TIME to 20 minutes, and press START.

5. When cooking cycle has finished, release pressure by carefully setting valve to EXHAUST on top of lid. Once all of pressure has released, turn lid, unlock, and open.

TIP *Instead of soaking beans overnight, add beans to the pressure cooker and cover with water by 1 inch. Pressure cook for 4 minutes and let the pressure drop naturally. Drain the beans and use in step 3 of the recipe.

Thanksgiving Turkey Soup

This soup is a great way to use up Thanksgiving leftovers, and will soon become a family favorite. Now, with the availability of the Great Flavors® Turkey Concentrate, you can have this nostalgic turkey-flavored soup any time of year.

Serves:
8

Prep Time:
15 minutes

Pressure Cooking Time:
10 minutes

Release Method:
QUICK

Ingredients:

2 pounds turkey tenderloin, cut into 1-inch pieces

Salt and pepper

1 tablespoon vegetable oil

2 medium sweet potatoes, peeled and cut into 1-inch pieces

2 stalks celery, chopped

1 medium onion, chopped

6 cups turkey broth, we recommend Great Flavors® Turkey Stock Concentrate

1 cup sweetened dried cranberries

2 tablespoons minced fresh sage

¼ teaspoon ground cinnamon

Directions:

1. Season turkey with salt and pepper. Add oil to inner pot. Set COOKING TIME to 15 minutes and press START. Heat oil 5 minutes. Add turkey and cook until browned, about 10 minutes. Press CANCEL.

2. Add sweet potato, celery, onion, broth, cranberries, sage, and cinnamon and stir to combine. Close and lock lid. Adjust pressure valve on top to AIRTIGHT, set COOKING TIME to 10 minutes, and press START.

3. When cooking cycle has finished, release pressure by carefully setting valve to EXHAUST on top of lid. Once all of pressure has released, turn lid, unlock, and open.

TIP Butternut squash or pumpkin can be substituted for the sweet potatoes. For a stuffing-like topping, add herbed croutons to individual bowls of soup.

Roma Tomato Soup

For Vegans and Vegetarians, the availability of Great Flavors® Vegetable Stock will make this fully vegetarian tomato soup a delicious lunchtime favorite. The addition of balsamic vinegar complements the sweetness of the tomatoes.

Serves:
8

Prep Time:
15 minutes

Pressure Cooking Time:
10 minutes

Release Method:
QUICK

Ingredients:

1 tablespoon unsalted butter

1 medium onion, chopped

2 pounds Roma tomatoes, cored and chopped

4 cups vegetable broth, we recommend Great Flavors® Vegetable Stock Concentrate

1 (6 oz.) can tomato paste

2 tablespoons balsamic vinegar

1 tablespoon Italian seasoning, we recommend Great Flavors® Italian Seasoning

1 tablespoon sugar

3 cloves garlic, minced

Salt and pepper

Directions:

1. Add butter to inner pot. Set COOKING TIME to 10 minutes and press START. Heat butter until melted, about 5 minutes. Add onion and cook until softened, about 5 minutes. Press CANCEL.

2. Add tomatoes, broth, tomato paste, vinegar, Italian seasoning, sugar, and garlic. Season with salt and pepper, and stir to combine. Close and lock lid. Adjust pressure valve on top to AIRTIGHT, set COOKING TIME to 10 minutes, and press START.

3. When cooking cycle has finished, release pressure by carefully setting valve to EXHAUST on top of lid. Once all of pressure has released, turn lid, unlock, and open.

4. Partially puree soup using a hand blender leaving as many chunks as you would like.

TIP For a creamy texture without added fat, add 4 slices white bread without the crust in step 2.

Serves:
6

Prep Time:
15 minutes

Pressure Cooking Time:
15 minutes

Release Method:
QUICK

Lentil Soup

Lentils are a great source of fiber and protein and literally soak up the flavors in this hearty, vegetarian soup. This is a great dish to cozy up to on a cold winter day. The best part is that the soup is ready in 30 minutes.

Ingredients:

1 tablespoon vegetable oil

1 medium onion, diced

1 large carrot, peeled and diced

1 stalk celery, diced

3 cloves garlic, minced

4 cups chicken broth, we recommend Great Flavors® Chicken Stock Concentrate

1 cup green or brown lentils

1 (15 oz.) can diced tomatoes, with liquid

2 bay leaves

¾ teaspoon dried thyme

¼ teaspoon ground cumin

3 cups chopped kale

1 teaspoon lemon juice

Salt and pepper

Directions:

1. Add oil to inner pot. Set COOKING TIME to 10 minutes and press START. Heat oil about 5 minutes. Add onion, carrot, celery, and garlic and cook until softened, about 5 minutes. Press CANCEL.

2. Add broth, lentils, diced tomato, bay leaves, thyme, cumin, kale, and lemon juice. Season with salt and pepper, and stir to combine.

3. Close and lock lid. Adjust pressure valve on top to AIRTIGHT, set COOKING TIME to 15 minutes, and press START. When cooking cycle has finished, release pressure by carefully setting valve to EXHAUST on top of lid. Once all of pressure has released, turn lid, unlock, and open. Season with salt and pepper.

TIP This recipe can be doubled easily. Add any chopped vegetables that you'd like in Step 2.

Italian Wedding Soup

Serves:
8

Prep Time:
15 minutes

Pressure
Cooking Time:
10 minutes

Release Method:
Quick

This traditional Italian soup is basically minestrone with added greens and meatballs. You can add almost any type of greens—spinach, escarole, beet greens, or kale.

Ingredients:

1 tablespoon vegetable oil

2 stalks celery, chopped

1 medium onion, chopped

1 large carrot, peeled and chopped

3 cloves garlic, minced

6 cups chicken broth, we recommend Great Flavors® Chicken Stock Concentrate

5 cups escarole or spinach, chopped

1 pound frozen mini meatballs, thawed

Salt and pepper

2 cups cooked Acini di Pepe pasta

1/3 cup grated Parmesan cheese

Directions:

1. Add oil to inner pot. Set COOKING TIME to 10 minutes and press START. Heat oil about 5 minutes. Add celery, onion, carrot, and garlic and cook until softened, about 5 minutes. Press CANCEL.

2. Add broth, escarole and meatballs. Season with salt and pepper, and stir to combine. Close and lock lid. Adjust pressure valve on top to AIRTIGHT, set COOKING TIME to 10 minutes, and press START.

3. When cooking cycle has finished, release pressure by carefully setting valve to EXHAUST on top of lid. Once all of pressure has released, turn lid, unlock, and open.

4. Add pasta and stir to combine. Serve, topped with Parmesan cheese.

TIP Any type of small pasta, such as orzo or stars, will work for this recipe. Cook the pasta separately or the starch from the pasta will make the broth cloudy.

Autumn Chicken Butternut Soup

Serves:
8

Prep Time:
15 minutes

Pressure Cooking Time:
10 minutes

Release Method:
QUICK

This is a very healthy comforting meal filled with warm root vegetables, white meat chicken, cumin, and cinnamon that combine to build great flavor. Guilt-free and delicious—what else could you ask for?

Ingredients:

1 tablespoon vegetable oil

2 medium onions, chopped

1 pound boneless, skinless chicken breast, cut into 1-inch pieces

1 pound butternut squash, peeled, cut into 1-inch pieces

2 medium parsnips, peeled, cut into 1-inch pieces

5 cups chicken broth, we recommend Great Flavors® Chicken Stock Concentrate

$\frac{1}{8}$ teaspoon ground cinnamon

$\frac{1}{4}$ teaspoon ground cumin

Salt and pepper

$\frac{1}{3}$ cup minced fresh parsley

Directions:

1. Add oil to inner pot. Set COOKING TIME to 10 minutes and press START. Heat oil about 5 minutes. Add onions and cook until softened, about 5 minutes. Press CANCEL.

2. Add chicken, butternut squash, parsnips, broth, cinnamon, and cumin. Season with salt and pepper. Stir to combine.

3. Close and lock lid. Adjust pressure valve on top to AIRTIGHT, set COOKING TIME to 10 minutes, and press START.

4. When cooking cycle has finished, release pressure by carefully setting valve to EXHAUST on top of lid. Once all of pressure has released, turn lid, unlock, and open. Add parsley.

TIP For a smooth vegetarian option, substitute vegetable broth for the chicken broth and omit the chicken. When the soup is done, cool and puree with a hand blender.

Cheeseburger Soup

Serves:
8

Prep Time:
15 minutes

Pressure Cooking Time:
10 minutes

Release Method:
QUICK

This recipe is based on a standard favorite—burger night! It has all the great fixings for a traditional cheeseburger with all the works, but now in a soup! Drizzle with ketchup, and serve with toasted hamburger buns and a side of pickles for a fun dinner with family or friends.

Ingredients:

2 pounds 95% lean ground beef

1 tablespoon steak seasoning

1 tablespoon vegetable oil

1 medium onion, chopped

3 cups beef broth, we recommend Great Flavors® Beef Stock Concentrate

1 (28 oz.) can diced tomatoes, drained

3 tablespoons steak sauce

3 cloves garlic, minced

1 (16 oz.) box pasteurized cheese, such as Velveeta®, cut into eighths

Directions:

1. Season beef with steak seasoning. Add oil to inner pot. Set COOKING TIME to 15 minutes and press START. Heat oil 5 minutes, then add seasoned ground beef to inner pot. Cook until browned, about 10 minutes. Press CANCEL.

2. Add onion, broth, tomatoes, steak sauce, and garlic and stir to combine. Close and lock lid. Adjust pressure valve on top to AIRTIGHT, set COOKING TIME to 10 minutes, and press START.

3. When cooking cycle has finished, release pressure by carefully setting valve to EXHAUST on top of lid. Once all of pressure has released, turn lid, unlock, and open.

4. Add pasteurized cheese and season with salt and pepper. Stir to combine.

TIP Adding your favorite burger cheese like Swiss or cheddar, and other typical burger accompaniments like mushrooms and bacon really personalize this soup.

Green Bean Casserole Soup

Serves:
8

Prep Time:
15 minutes

Pressure
Cooking Time:
10 minutes

Release Method:
QUICK

Your favorite Thanksgiving classic has now transformed into a warm comforting soup. Mushrooms, green beans, onion, sage, and thyme blend together for a tasty, one-of-a-kind soup experience. Cooking the onion first adds tremendous flavor.

Ingredients:

1 tablespoon vegetable oil

1 medium onion, chopped

¾ pound white mushrooms, trimmed and halved

1 ½ pounds frozen cut green beans, thawed

4 cups vegetable broth, we recommend Great Flavors® Vegetable Stock Concentrate

1 tablespoon minced fresh sage

1 tablespoon minced fresh thyme

Salt and pepper

1 cup milk

4 tablespoons cornstarch mixed with ¼ cup milk

1 (2.8 oz.) container French fried onions

Directions:

1. Add oil to inner pot. Set COOKING TIME to 10 minutes and press START. Heat oil about 5 minutes. Add onions to inner pot and cook until softened, about 5 minutes. Press CANCEL.

2. Add mushrooms, green beans, broth, sage, and thyme. Season with salt and pepper. Close and lock lid. Adjust pressure valve on top to AIRTIGHT, set COOKING TIME to 10 minutes, and press START.

3. When cooking cycle has finished, release pressure by carefully setting valve to EXHAUST on top of lid. Once all of pressure has released, turn lid, unlock, and open.

4. Set COOKING TIME to 3 minutes and press START. Add milk and cornstarch mixture and stir to combine. Serve, topped with French fried onions.

TIP Not a fan of green beans? This soup can be made with broccoli, corn, potatoes, chicken, or celery.

Super Fine Chicken Noodle Soup

Serves:
8

Prep Time:
15 minutes

Pressure Cooking Time:
10 minutes

Release Method:
QUICK

An interesting trick is to add fresh parsley and dill to your chicken soup to give it amazing flavor. Your family will always feel better after a bowl of this special soup. In addition, this recipe is super fine because of the additional flavor from leeks and root vegetables.

Ingredients:

2 pounds boneless, skinless chicken breast, cut into 1-inch pieces

Salt and pepper

1 tablespoon vegetable oil

2 stalks celery, chopped

1 medium leek, cleaned and chopped

1 large carrot, peeled and chopped

1 large parsnip, peeled and chopped

8 cups chicken broth, we recommend Great Flavors® Chicken Stock Concentrate

¼ cup minced fresh parsley

2 tablespoons minced fresh dill

2 cups cooked fine egg noodles

Directions:

1. Season chicken with salt and pepper. Add oil to inner pot. Set COOKING TIME to 15 minutes and press START. Heat oil about 5 minutes. Add chicken to inner pot and cook until browned, about 10 minutes. Press CANCEL.

2. Add celery, leek, carrot, parsnip, broth, parsley, and dill and stir to combine. Close and lock lid. Adjust pressure valve on top to AIRTIGHT, set COOKING TIME to 10 minutes, and press START.

3. When cooking cycle has finished, release pressure by carefully setting valve to EXHAUST on top of lid. Once all of pressure has released, turn lid, unlock, and open.

4. Add egg noodles and serve.

TIP If you're going to freeze the soup, don't add the noodles. As they sit in the soup they will soak up too much broth. Instead, add the noodles to individual servings.

Chunky Minestrone Barley Soup

Serves:
8

Prep Time:
15 minutes

Pressure Cooking Time:
20 minutes

Release Method:
QUICK

Healthy AND Delicious? Yes! This recipe combines fresh vegetables you most likely have on hand. Using the pressure cooker, we can also add whole grains, such as barley, and still get soup on the table in about 30 minutes. The nutty flavor and texture of barley makes this soup uniquely satisfying.

Ingredients:

1 tablespoon vegetable oil

2 medium carrots, peeled and chopped

2 stalks celery, chopped

1 medium onion, chopped

3 cups vegetable broth, we recommend Great Flavors® Vegetable Stock Concentrate

1 (28 oz.) can diced tomatoes

3 cups fresh spinach leaves, chopped

3 tablespoons tomato paste

1 cup uncooked barley

1 tablespoon Italian seasoning, we recommend Great Flavors® Italian Seasoning

Salt and pepper

1 (14.5 oz.) can kidney beans, drained and rinsed

Directions:

1. Add oil to inner pot. Set COOKING TIME to 10 minutes and press START. Heat oil about 5 minute. Add carrot, celery, and onion and cook until softened, about 5 minutes. Press CANCEL.

2. Add broth, diced tomato, spinach, tomato paste, barley, and Italian seasoning. Season with salt and pepper. Stir to combine. Close and lock lid. Adjust pressure valve on top to AIRTIGHT, set COOKING TIME to 20 minutes, and press START.

3. When cooking cycle has finished, release pressure by carefully setting valve to EXHAUST on top of lid. Once all of pressure has released, turn lid, unlock, and open.

4. Add kidney beans and stir to combine.

TIP Minestrone soup can be made with whichever vegetables or protein you have available.

Loaded Potato Chowder

Serves:
6 to 8

Prep Time:
20 minutes

Pressure Cooking Time:
10 minutes

Release Method:
QUICK

Cooking the bacon first adds such rich flavor to this soup. This fully loaded chowder is quick and easy to make, and will add to any meal, or stand on its own with an extra-large serving.

Ingredients:

1 tablespoons vegetable oil

½ pound bacon, cut into ½-inch pieces

2 stalks celery, chopped

1 medium onion, chopped

4 cups chicken broth, we recommend Great Flavors® Chicken Stock Concentrate

2 pounds potatoes, peeled, cut into ¾-inch pieces

Salt and pepper

¾ cup heavy cream

1 teaspoon Old Bay® Seasoning

1 cup shredded cheddar cheese

¼ cup minced fresh chives

Directions:

1. Add oil to pot. Set COOKING TIME to 20 minutes and press START. Heat oil about 5 minutes. Add bacon to inner pot, cook until browned, about 10 minutes. Remove bacon and set aside. Add celery and onion and cook until softened, about 5 minutes. Press CANCEL.

2. Add broth and potatoes. Season with salt and pepper. Close and lock lid. Adjust pressure valve on top to AIRTIGHT, set COOKING TIME to 10 minutes, and press START.

3. When cooking cycle has finished, release pressure by carefully setting valve to EXHAUST on top of lid. Once all of pressure has released, turn lid, unlock, and open.

4. Stir in heavy cream and Old Bay Seasoning. Partially puree soup using a hand blender or mash with potato masher. Serve each bowl of soup topped with cheese, chives, and cooked bacon.

TIP Any type of potato will work in this recipe. To make this into potato corn chowder, simply add 2 cups thawed corn kernels after pureeing the soup in Step 4.

POULTRY

Turkey Pot Pie, 69

Beer Can Chicken

Serves:
6

Prep Time:
20 minutes

Pressure
Cooking Time:
20 minutes

Release Method:
QUICK

This whole, spiced chicken emerges from the pressure cooker in less than a half an hour moist and full of flavor, thanks to the the beer that is added to the pot. Other than an IPA, which can be too bitter when cooked, use any style of beer you have on hand.

Ingredients:

1 (5 to 5 $\frac{1}{2}$ lb.) whole chicken

2 tablespoons minced fresh rosemary

1 teaspoon paprika

1 teaspoon ground ginger

Salt and pepper

2 tablespoons vegetable oil

2 (12 oz.) cans beer

Directions:

1. Rinse chicken in cold water and pat dry. In a small bowl, combine rosemary, paprika, ginger, 1 teaspoon salt, and $\frac{1}{2}$ teaspoon pepper. Season chicken with herb mixture.

2. Add oil to inner pot. Set COOKING TIME to 15 minutes and press START. Heat oil about 5 minutes. Add chicken and cook until browned, about 10 minutes. Press CANCEL.

3. Add beer. Close and lock lid. Adjust pressure valve on top to AIRTIGHT, set COOKING TIME to 20 minutes, and press START.

4. When cooking cycle has finished, release pressure by carefully setting valve to EXHAUST on top of lid. Once all of pressure has released, turn lid, unlock, and open.

TIP For crispy skin, place chicken on a foil-lined pan and place under the broiler until crispy, 5 to 7 minutes.

Take-Out Thai Chicken

You can make this recipe healthier, and even tastier, by swapping yogurt for dairy. Yogurt mingles wonderfully with the Thai flavors of coconut milk, cilantro, and curry.

Serves:
8

Prep Time:
15 minutes

Pressure Cooking Time:
13 minutes

Release Method:
QUICK

Ingredients:

2 pounds boneless, skinless chicken breast, cut into 1-inch chunks

Salt and pepper

1 tablespoon vegetable oil

1 medium onion, sliced thin

1 cup coconut milk

1 (14.5 oz.) can stewed tomatoes

2 tablespoons curry powder

1 cup plain Greek yogurt

1 tablespoon cornstarch

¼ cup chopped fresh cilantro

Directions:

1. Season chicken with salt and pepper. Add oil to inner pot. Set COOKING TIME to 15 minutes and press START. Heat oil about 5 minutes. Add chicken and cook until browned, about 10 minutes. Press CANCEL.

2. Add onion, coconut milk, tomatoes, and curry and stir to combine. Close and lock lid. Adjust pressure valve on top to AIRTIGHT, set COOKING TIME to 10 minutes, and press START.

3. When cooking cycle has finished, release pressure by carefully setting valve to EXHAUST on top of lid. Once all of pressure has released, turn lid, unlock, and open.

4. In a small bowl, combine yogurt and cornstarch.

5. Set COOKING TIME to 3 minutes and press START. Add yogurt mixture and stir to combine. Cook until thickened, about 3 minutes. Season with salt and pepper. Sprinkle with cilantro.

TIP **This dish goes great with our Brown Rice Pilaf on page 132.**

Chicken & Dumplings

Pressure-cooked chicken and dumplings is the ultimate in comfort food meals. It always creates warmth, and a sense of commitment and well-being around the kitchen table with family.

Serves:
8

Prep Time:
20 minutes

Pressure Cooking Time:
45 minutes

Release Method:
QUICK

Ingredients:

CHICKEN

2 pounds chicken tenderloin, cut into 1-inch pieces

4 tablespoons unsalted butter

2 stalks celery, chopped

2 medium carrots, peeled and sliced

1 medium onion, chopped

4 tablespoons all-purpose flour

3 ½ cups chicken broth, we recommend Great Flavors® Chicken Stock Concentrate

3 cloves garlic, minced

1 tablespoon minced fresh thyme

1 cup frozen peas, thawed

½ cup heavy cream

Salt and pepper

BISCUITS

2 cups Bisquick®

⅔ cup milk

2 teaspoons minced fresh thyme

Directions:

1. Add butter to inner pot. Set COOKING TIME to 20 minutes and press START. Heat butter until melted, about 5 minutes. Add chicken and cook until browned, about 10 minutes. Add celery, carrots, and onion and cook until just softened, about 3 minutes. Add flour and cook, stirring, until incorporated, about 2 minutes. Press CANCEL.

2. Add broth, garlic, and thyme and stir to combine. Close and lock lid. Adjust pressure valve on top to AIRTIGHT, set COOKING TIME to 15 minutes, and press START.

3. When cooking cycle has finished, release pressure by carefully setting valve to EXHAUST on top of lid. Once all of pressure has released, turn lid, unlock, and open.

4. In a medium bowl, combine Bisquick, milk, and thyme.

5. With the cooker's lid off, set COOKING TIME to 10 minutes and press START. Add peas and heavy cream. Season with salt and pepper and stir to combine.

6. Drop spoonfuls of biscuit dough on top of chicken mixture. Cover, unlocked, and simmer until biscuits are cooked through and fluffy.

TIP **To make an even easier dumpling, use uncooked refrigerated biscuits in place of the Bisquick®.**

Chicken with Mushroom Gravy

Serves:
8

Prep Time:
15 minutes

Pressure Cooking Time:
12 minutes

Release Method:
QUICK

A classic American comfort food, this is now a fast, simple main dish prepared in just minutes. You can make many variations by changing the spices and mushrooms, which you select. For an Italian flavor profile, try Great Flavors® Italian Seasoning instead of the sage.

Ingredients:

8 (6 oz.) boneless, skinless chicken breast

Salt and pepper

1 tablespoon vegetable oil

1 medium red onion, sliced thin

1 pound medium mushrooms, cut in half

1 cup red wine

1 cup chicken broth, we recommend Great Flavors® Chicken Stock Concentrate

2 tablespoons minced fresh sage

2 tablespoons cornstarch mixed with ¼ cup milk

2 tablespoons unsalted butter

Directions:

1. Season chicken with salt and pepper. Add oil to inner pot. Set COOKING TIME to 15 minutes and press START. Heat oil about 5 minutes. Add chicken and cook until browned, about 10 minutes. Press CANCEL.

2. Add onion, mushrooms, wine, broth, and sage and stir to combine. Close and lock lid. Adjust pressure valve on top to AIRTIGHT, set COOKING TIME to 10 minutes, and press START.

3. When cooking cycle has finished, release pressure by carefully setting valve to EXHAUST on top of lid. Once all of pressure has released, turn lid, unlock, and open.

4. Transfer chicken to serving dish. With the cooker's lid off, set COOKING TIME to 2 minutes and press START. Add cornstarch mixture and butter to remaining sauce, and stir to combine. Cook until sauce thickens.

TIP Domestic white mushrooms have a delicate flavor. For more woodsy and meaty flavor, try using a variety of more exotic mushrooms.

Honey Lime Chicken

The combination of lime and honey makes this recipe at once sweet and sour. The crushed red pepper flakes add heat that adds a nice kick at the end of each bite. The pressure cooker cooks chicken to moist and tender perfection.

Serves:
8

Prep Time:
15 minutes

Pressure Cooking Time:
12 minutes

Release Method:
QUICK

Ingredients:

8 (6 oz.) boneless, skinless chicken breast

Salt and pepper

1 tablespoon vegetable oil

1 cup chicken broth, we recommend Great Flavors® Chicken Stock Concentrate

¼ cup whole grain mustard

¼ cup lime juice

3 tablespoons honey

½ teaspoon crushed red pepper flakes

2 tablespoons cornstarch mixed with ¼ cup water

Directions:

1. Season chicken with salt and pepper. Add oil to inner pot. Set COOKING TIME to 15 minutes and press START. Heat oil about 5 minutes. Add chicken and cook until browned, about 10 minutes. Press CANCEL.

2. Add broth, mustard, lime juice, honey, and crushed red pepper flakes and stir to combine. Close and lock lid. Adjust pressure valve on top to AIRTIGHT, set COOKING TIME to 10 minutes, and press START.

3. When cooking cycle has finished, release pressure by carefully setting valve to EXHAUST on top of lid. Once all of pressure has released, turn lid, unlock, and open.

4. Transfer chicken to serving dish. Set COOKING TIME to 2 minutes and press START. Add cornstarch mixture and stir to combine. Cook until sauce thickens, about 2 minutes. Season with salt and pepper.

TIP For extra lime zip, zest 2 fresh limes before juicing and add zest in Step 4.

Pesto Chicken Pasta

Serves:
8

Prep Time:
5 minutes

Pressure
Cooking Time:
8 minutes +
5 minute rest

Release Method:
QUICK

Cavatappi means corkscrew in Italian, and is literally twisted elbow macaroni with ridges, which catch any delicious sauce. As a result, the Alfredo sauce collects in each crevice for a mouthful of flavor in every bite.

Ingredients:

1 (15 oz.) jar Alfredo sauce

2 ¼ cups water

1 cup basil pesto

10 ounces cavatappi pasta

1 pound frozen grilled chicken strips

½ teaspoon pepper

Directions:

1. Add all ingredients to inner pot and stir to combine, ensuring pasta is below water level. Close and lock lid. Adjust pressure valve on top to AIRTIGHT, set COOKING TIME to 8 minutes, and press START.

2. When cooking cycle has finished, release pressure by carefully setting valve to EXHAUST on top of lid. Once all of pressure has released, turn lid, unlock, and open.

3. Let pasta rest in the pressure cooker with the lid closed for 5 minutes.

4. Transfer to serving dish.

TIP Try adding additional ingredients such as cooked bacon, cherry tomatoes, or spinach in Step 3.

Serves:
8

Prep Time:
15 minutes

Pressure Cooking Time:
10 minutes

Release Method:
QUICK

Chicken with Broccoli Cheese Sauce

You can make this fast and easy recipe entirely from ingredients in your pantry and freezer in less than 30 minutes. If you like broccoli with cheese, this will become a go-to favorite. It's a great way to serve one of the world's healthiest vegetables.

Ingredients:

8 (6 oz.) boneless, skinless chicken breast

Salt and pepper

1 tablespoon vegetable oil

1 ½ cups milk

1 (10.75 oz.) can cheddar cheese soup

½ pound frozen chopped broccoli

1 cup shredded cheddar cheese

1 ¼ cups crushed buttery crackers, such as Ritz®

Directions:

1. Season chicken with salt and pepper. Add oil to inner pot. Set COOKING TIME to 15 minutes and press START. Heat oil about 5 minutes. Add chicken and cook until browned, about 10 minutes. Press CANCEL.

2. Add milk, soup, broccoli, and cheese and stir to combine. Close and lock lid. Adjust pressure valve on top to AIRTIGHT, set COOKING TIME to 10 minutes, and press START.

3. When cooking cycle has finished, release pressure by carefully setting valve to EXHAUST on top of lid. Once all of pressure has released, turn lid, unlock, and open.

4. Transfer chicken and sauce to serving dish and top with crushed crackers.

TIP To enjoy all of the cheesy sauce, serve with a loaf of your favorite crusty bread.

Maple & Mustard Glazed Chicken

Serves:
8

Prep Time:
15 minutes

Pressure Cooking Time:
12 minutes

Release Method:
QUICK

Sweet and savory marinades provide great flavor for leaner meats. The pressure cooker does a great job adding flavor and keeping chicken moist and delicious. The sweetness of the maple syrup balances the tangy flavors of the mustard and vinegar. Plus, dinner is done in less than 30 minutes!

Ingredients:

8 (6 oz.) boneless, skinless chicken breasts

Salt and pepper

1 tablespoon vegetable oil

1 cup chicken broth, we recommend Great Flavors® Chicken Stock Concentrate

2 cloves garlic, minced

⅓ cup maple syrup

¼ cup Dijon mustard

1 tablespoon red wine vinegar

½ teaspoon dried tarragon

1 teaspoon cornstarch mixed with 2 tablespoons water

Directions:

1. Season chicken with salt and pepper. Add oil to inner pot. Set COOKING TIME to 15 minutes and press START. Heat oil about 5 minutes. Add chicken and cook until browned, about 10 minutes. Press CANCEL.

2. Add broth, garlic, maple syrup, mustard, vinegar, and tarragon and stir to combine. Close and lock lid. Adjust pressure valve on top to AIRTIGHT, set COOKING TIME to 10 minutes, and press START.

3. When cooking cycle has finished, release pressure by carefully setting valve to EXHAUST on top of lid. Once all of pressure has released, turn lid, unlock, and open.

4. Transfer chicken to serving dish. Set COOKING TIME to 2 minutes and press START. Add cornstarch mixture and stir to combine. Cook until sauce thickens, about 2 minutes.

TIP Try using other types of mustard such as whole grain, spicy brown, or yellow. Each will result in its own unique taste.

Amazing Apricot Chicken

Serves:
8

Prep Time:
15 minutes

Pressure Cooking Time:
12 minutes

Release Method:
QUICK

Our recipe testers voted this recipe, "Best of Chicken." Not only does the combination of apricot preserves, fresh apricots, soy, garlic and mustard taste terrific, but the finished product looks beautiful on the plate as well. It will draw rave reviews, and you will have it on the table in less than 30 minutes.

Ingredients:

8 (6 oz.) boneless, skinless chicken breast

Salt and pepper

1 tablespoon vegetable oil

2 tablespoon soy sauce

2 cloves garlic, minced

1 tablespoon light brown sugar

6 dried apricots, diced

4 teaspoons fresh lemon juice

½ cup apricot preserves

1 teaspoon Dijon mustard

1 teaspoon cornstarch, mixed with 2 tablespoons water

Directions:

1. Season chicken with salt and pepper. Add oil to inner pot. Set COOKING TIME to 15 minutes and press START. Heat oil about 5 minutes. Add chicken and cook until browned, about 10 minutes. Press CANCEL.

2. Add soy sauce, garlic, brown sugar, apricots, and lemon juice and stir to combine. Close and lock lid. Adjust pressure valve on top to AIRTIGHT, set COOKING TIME to 10 minutes, and press START.

3. When cooking cycle has finished, release pressure by carefully setting valve to EXHAUST on top of lid. Once all of pressure has released, turn lid, unlock, and open.

4. In a small bowl, combine apricot preserves, mustard, and cornstarch mixture.

5. Set COOKING TIME to 2 minutes and press START. Add apricot mixture and stir to combine. Cook until thickened, about 2 minutes. Season with salt and pepper.

TIP For enhanced flavor and crunch, top each chicken breast with sliced toasted almonds and a pinch of cardamom.

Balsamic Marinated Chicken Thighs

Serves:
8

Prep Time:
15 minutes +
4 hour marinade

Pressure
Cooking Time:
15 minutes

Release Method:
QUICK

Chicken thighs can be purchased in bulk, and are one of the best protein values available. In a pressure cooker they become tender mouthfuls of dark meat. This recipe bathes the chicken in a tangy, sweet balsamic marinade.

Ingredients:

2 ½ to 3 pounds bone in, skinless chicken thighs

1 (16 oz.) bottle balsamic vinaigrette

2 tablespoons vegetable oil

1 cup chicken broth, we recommend Great Flavors® Chicken Stock Concentrate

1 tablespoon minced fresh rosemary

Directions:

1. Place chicken thighs and vinaigrette in an airtight container and refrigerate for 4 hours or overnight. Remove chicken from marinade and pat dry.

2. Add oil to inner pot. Set COOKING TIME to 15 minutes and press START. Heat oil about 5 minutes. Add chicken and cook until browned, about 10 minutes. Press CANCEL.

3. Add broth and rosemary. Close and lock lid. Adjust pressure valve on top to AIRTIGHT, set COOKING TIME to 15 minutes, and press START.

4. When cooking cycle has finished, release pressure by carefully setting valve to EXHAUST on top of lid. Once all of pressure has released, turn lid, unlock, and open. Season with salt and pepper.

TIP For a lighter dish, serve the chicken with your favorite greens and use the cooking liquid as a warm salad dressing. To make the dressing, whisk ¼ cup cooking liquid, 3 tablespoons extra-virgin olive oil, and 4 teaspoons lemon juice in small bowl.

Fall Off the Bone Chicken

It is best to cook these chicken legs for 30 minutes, because they will then be falling-off-the-bone tender. The dark meat will absorb the flavor during the last five minutes, and you will be rewarded with fantastic taste and texture.

Serves:
8

Prep Time:
10 minutes

Pressure Cooking Time:
30 minutes

Release Method:
Quick

Ingredients:

4 pounds skinless chicken leg quarters

Salt and pepper

1 cup chicken broth, we recommend Great Flavors® Chicken Stock Concentrate

1 cup pitted green olives

2 cloves garlic, minced

3 tablespoons unsalted butter

3 tablespoons fresh lemon juice

1 tablespoon fennel seeds

1 teaspoon dried oregano

Directions:

1. Season chicken with salt and pepper. Add all ingredients to inner pot. Close and lock lid. Adjust pressure valve on top to AIRTIGHT, set COOKING TIME to 30 minutes, and press START.

2. When cooking cycle has finished, release pressure by carefully setting valve to EXHAUST on top of lid. Once all of pressure has released, turn lid, unlock, and open.

TIP Any spices in this recipe can be replaced with your favorite seasoning.

Skinny Chicken Parmesan

Serves:
8

Prep Time:
15 minutes

Pressure Cooking Time:
10 minutes

Release Method:
QUICK

What makes this recipe Skinny? By eliminating the breadcrumbs, you eliminate over 100 calories from each serving. Now, the Parmesan and chicken really stand out. You will love this lighter version of the Italian classic.

Ingredients:

8 (6 oz.) boneless, skinless chicken breast

Salt and pepper

1 tablespoon vegetable oil

1 medium onion, chopped

4 cloves garlic, minced

1 can (14 oz.) crushed tomatoes

½ cup red wine

1 tablespoon sugar

1 cup grated Parmesan cheese

¼ cup minced fresh basil

Directions:

1. Season chicken with salt and pepper. Add oil to inner pot. Set COOKING TIME to 15 minutes and press START. Heat oil about 5 minutes. Add chicken and cook until browned, about 10 minutes. Press CANCEL.

2. Add onion, garlic, tomatoes, wine, and sugar and stir to combine. Close and lock lid. Adjust pressure valve on top to AIRTIGHT, set COOKING TIME to 10 minutes, and press START.

3. When cooking cycle has finished, release pressure by carefully setting valve to EXHAUST on top of lid. Once all of pressure has released, turn lid, unlock, and open.

4. Transfer chicken to serving dish and season sauce with salt and pepper. Top chicken with sauce and sprinkle with Parmesan and basil.

TIP Add a side of your favorite style of pasta, if you'd like. This recipe makes enough sauce to top the chicken and a side of pasta.

Serves:
8

Prep Time:
15 minutes

Pressure Cooking Time:
12 minutes

Release Method:
QUICK

 # Orange Peel Chicken

"Sweet and Heat" is the best way to describe this tasty orange-flavored chicken. The heat is from the pervading zest of Sriracha sauce and ginger and the sweet is provided by the orange marmalade. This is another great example of how the pressure cooker infuses flavor deep into the meat. Yum, Yum!

Ingredients:

3 pounds boneless, skinless chicken breast, cut into 1-inch pieces

Salt and pepper

1 tablespoon vegetable oil

1 (8 oz.) can tomato sauce

1 orange, peeled, peel reserved plus ⅓ cup juice

⅓ cup orange marmalade

¼ cup soy sauce

1 tablespoon Sriracha sauce

2 cloves garlic, minced

3 tablespoons cornstarch mixed with ¼ cup water

4 green onions, chopped

Directions:

1. Season chicken with salt and pepper. Add oil to inner pot. Set COOKING TIME to 15 minutes and press START. Heat oil about 5 minutes. Add chicken and cook until browned, about 10 minutes. Press CANCEL.

2. Add tomato sauce, orange juice, marmalade, soy sauce, Sriracha, and garlic and stir to combine. Close and lock lid. Adjust pressure valve on top to AIRTIGHT, set COOKING TIME to 10 minutes, and press START. While chicken is cooking, thinly slice reserved orange peel.

3. When cooking cycle has finished, release pressure by carefully setting valve to EXHAUST on top of lid. Once all of pressure has released, turn lid, unlock, and open.

4. Transfer chicken to serving dish. With the cooker's lid off, set COOKING TIME to 2 minutes and press START. Add cornstarch mixture, orange peel, and green onions and stir to combine. Cook until sauce thickens.

TIP To make apricot-orange chicken, substitute apricot preserves for the orange marmalade.

General Tso's Chicken

Serves:
8

Prep Time:
15 minutes

Pressure Cooking Time:
12 minutes

Release Method:
QUICK

This popular Chinese dish is named after General Tso Tsung-tang, or Zuo Zongtang, a Qing Dynasty general and statesman. Instead of opting for a fried take-out version, you can make this homemade pressure-infused version in less than 30 minutes.

Ingredients:

3 pounds boneless, skinless chicken breast, cut into 1-inch pieces

Salt and pepper

1 tablespoon vegetable oil

⅓ cup light brown sugar

⅓ cup low-sodium soy sauce

¼ cup rice vinegar

¼ cup hoisin sauce

6 dried red chilies, chopped

4 cloves garlic, minced

2 tablespoons minced fresh ginger

3 tablespoons cornstarch mixed with ¼ cup water

8 green onions, chopped

Directions:

1. Season chicken with salt and pepper. Add oil to inner pot. Set COOKING TIME to 15 minutes and press START. Heat oil about 5 minutes. Add chicken and cook until browned, about 10 minutes. Press CANCEL.

2. Add brown sugar, soy sauce, vinegar, hoisin, chilies, garlic, and ginger and stir to combine. Close and lock lid. Adjust pressure valve on top to AIRTIGHT, set COOKING TIME to 10 minutes, and press START.

3. When cooking cycle has finished, release pressure by carefully setting valve to EXHAUST on top of lid. Once all of pressure has released, turn lid, unlock, and open.

4. With the cooker's lid off, set COOKING TIME to 2 minutes and press START. Add cornstarch mixture and stir to combine. Cook until sauce thickens, and garnish with green onions.

TIP For a vegetarian version, substitute extra-firm tofu for the chicken.

Fajita-Seasoned Chicken Breasts

Serves:
8

Prep Time:
15 minutes

Pressure
Cooking Time:
10 minutes

Release Method:
QUICK

You will love this chicken recipe, because you can use the chicken in so many different ways—in tacos, quesadillas, fajitas, pulled chicken or chicken salad sandwiches, and a host of your own ideas. Make this ahead and keep a batch in the refrigerator or freezer for last-minute meals.

Ingredients:

8 (6 oz.) boneless, skinless chicken breast

1 (1 oz.) packet fajita seasoning mix

1 tablespoon vegetable oil

1 green bell pepper, seeded and sliced thin

1 red bell pepper, seeded and sliced thin

1 medium onion, sliced thin

½ cup chicken broth, we recommend Great Flavors® Chicken Stock Concentrate

1 cup shredded Monterey jack cheese

Directions:

1. Season chicken with fajita seasoning mix. Add oil to inner pot. Set COOKING TIME to 15 minutes and press START. Heat oil about 5 minutes. Add chicken and cook until browned, about 10 minutes. Press CANCEL.

2. Add peppers, onion, and broth and stir to combine. Close and lock lid. Adjust pressure valve on top to AIRTIGHT, set COOKING TIME to 10 minutes, and press START.

3. When cooking cycle has finished, release pressure by carefully setting valve to EXHAUST on top of lid. Once all of pressure has released, turn lid, unlock, and open.

4. Transfer chicken, peppers, and onion to serving dish, and top with cheese.

TIP **This dish can be served over rice. Or, shred the chicken and serve in warm flour tortillas topped with peppers, onions, and cheese.**

Turkey Pot Pie

Serves:
12

Prep Time:
45 minutes

Cook Time:
15 minutes

Release Method:
QUICK

Originally this was a leftover family favorite that was only made on the day after Thanksgiving and Christmas. Now, with turkey breast available year round, you are only a few minutes away from this yummy comfort food any day of the week.

Ingredients:

1 box frozen puff pastry sheets, thawed

1 egg mixed with 1 tablespoon water

2 tablespoons unsalted butter

1½ pounds fresh turkey breast, cut into 1-inch pieces

Salt and pepper

4 medium red potatoes, cubed

2 medium carrots, peeled and chopped

1 medium onion, chopped

2 cups turkey broth, we recommend Great Flavors® Turkey Stock Concentrate

2 tablespoons minced fresh thyme

1 teaspoon sugar

¾ teaspoon poultry seasoning

1 cup frozen peas, thawed

¾ cup instant potato flakes

½ cup heavy cream

¼ cup grated Parmesan cheese

Directions:

1. Cut each sheet of thawed puff pastry into 6 portions. Brush with egg mixture. Follow baking instructions on puff pastry package instructions.

2. Season turkey with salt and pepper. Add butter to inner pot. Set COOKING TIME to 15 minutes and press START. Heat butter until melted, about 5 minutes. Add turkey and cook until browned, about 10 minutes. Press CANCEL.

3. Add potatoes, carrots, onion, broth, thyme, sugar, and poultry seasoning and stir to combine. Close and lock lid. Adjust pressure valve on top to AIRTIGHT, set COOKING TIME to 10 minutes, and press START.

4. When cooking cycle has finished, release pressure by carefully setting valve to EXHAUST on top of lid. Once all of pressure has released, turn lid, unlock, and open.

5. Set COOKING TIME to 5 minutes and press START. With cooker's lid off, add peas, potato flakes, heavy cream, and Parmesan and stir to combine. Cook until heated through, about 5 minutes. Serve, topped with puff pastry.

Smoked Chicken Legs

Serves:
8

Prep Time:
15 minutes

Pressure Cooking Time:
50 minutes (includes pressure release time)

Release Method:
NATURAL

Which would you rather—spending hours smoking chicken over a hot grill or getting the same result from thirty minutes in the pressure cooker? That's what we thought. The addition of cranberries and walnuts develop a sauce with deep, earthy flavor.

Ingredients:

3 pounds skinless chicken legs

1 tablespoon vegetable oil

Salt and pepper

1 cup chicken broth, we recommend Great Flavors® Chicken Stock Concentrate

1 medium onion, sliced thin

1 cup frozen cranberries

1 cup walnuts

1 tablespoon smoked paprika

1 tablespoon minced fresh thyme

Directions:

1. Season chicken with salt and pepper. Add oil to inner pot. Set COOKING TIME to 15 minutes and press START. Heat oil about 5 minutes. Add chicken legs and cook until browned, about 10 minutes. Press CANCEL.

2. Add broth, onion, cranberries, walnuts, paprika, and thyme and stir to combine. Close and lock lid. Adjust pressure valve on top to AIRTIGHT, set COOKING TIME to 30 minutes, and press START.

3. When cooking cycle has finished, let pressure drop NATURALLY. Once all of pressure has released, turn lid, unlock, and open.

TIP For a variation on this recipe, try turkey legs when they are available around the holidays.

BEEF

Corned Beef in Dijon Sauce, 91

Pizza Stuffed Meatloaf

Your meatloaf will never be bland again. Each slice is filled with flavorful herbs, peppers, and pepperoni and finished off with a center of melted mozzarella. Serve with the sauce on top of each slice.

Serves:
6 to 8

Prep Time:
30 minutes

Pressure Cooking Time:
20 minutes +
5 minutes rest

Release Method:
QUICK

Ingredients:

1 ¼ **pounds 95% lean ground beef**

⅓ **cup Italian bread crumbs**

2 **large eggs**

1 **medium onion, minced**

1 **tablespoon Italian seasoning, we recommend Great Flavors® Italian Seasoning**

2 **cloves garlic, minced**

Salt and pepper

2 **cups shredded mozzarella cheese, divided**

1 **red bell pepper, diced**

½ **cup diced pepperoni**

1 **tablespoon vegetable oil**

1 **(14 oz.) jar pizza sauce**

Directions:

1. In a large bowl, combine ground beef, bread crumbs, eggs, onion, Italian seasoning and garlic. Season with salt and pepper.

2. On a piece of plastic wrap, flatten ground beef mixture to 8-inch x 10-inch rectangle. Place 1 cup mozzarella cheese, red peppers, and pepperoni in the middle crosswise. Starting from the short side, fold, forming a loaf making sure all edges are sealed.

3. Add oil to inner pot and add meatloaf. Top with pizza sauce. Close and lock lid. Adjust pressure valve on top to AIRTIGHT, set COOKING TIME to 20 minutes, and press START.

4. When cooking cycle has finished, release pressure by carefully setting valve to EXHAUST on top of lid. Once all of pressure has released, turn lid, unlock, and open.

5. Top with remaining mozzarella cheese. Let rest, covered, for 5 minutes or until cheese is melted.

TIP **Equal quantities of your favorite pizza toppings, such as black olives, cooked mushrooms, or cooked bacon can be substituted for the red pepper or pepperoni.**

Serves:
8

Prep Time:
30 minutes

Pressure Cooking Time:
20 minutes +
5 minutes rest

Release Method:
QUICK

Mini Meatloaves

This is a great weekday dinner staple, and is so simple to make. Simply mix the beef with flavorful ingredients, form into loaves, and cook for 20 minutes. Serve with your favorite vegetables and some mashed potatoes, and dinner is on the table in no time!

Ingredients:

2 ½ pounds 95% lean ground beef

¾ cup Italian bread crumbs

3 large eggs

1 medium onion, minced

1 tablespoon Worcestershire sauce

1 tablespoon Italian seasoning, we recommend Great Flavors® Italian Seasoning

½ cup minced fresh parsley

3 cloves garlic, minced

Salt and pepper

1 cup ketchup

½ cup beef broth, we recommend Great Flavors® Beef Stock Concentrate

Directions:

1. In a large bowl, combine ground beef, bread crumbs, eggs, onion, Worcestershire, Italian seasoning, parsley, and garlic, 1 teaspoon salt, and ½ teaspoon pepper. Divide mixture in half and form into 2 loaves.

2. Spray inner pot with nonstick cooking spray. Place loaves in pot. Add ketchup and broth. Close and lock lid. Adjust pressure valve on top to AIRTIGHT, set COOKING TIME to 20 minutes, and press START.

3. When cooking cycle has finished, release pressure by carefully setting valve to EXHAUST on top of lid. Once all of pressure has released, turn lid, unlock, and open.

4. Remove meatloaf and let rest, covered with aluminum foil, for 5 minutes before carving and serving.

TIP Nothing pairs better with meatloaf than mashed potatoes. See our recipe for Classic Mashed Potatoes on page 154.

Mongolian Beef

The sauce in this dish makes this meal really special. The combination of sesame oil, hoisin sauce, soy sauce, crushed red pepper, garlic and ginger creates the perfect balance of sweet, savory, and spicy. This sauce works well with chicken and pork too!

Serves:
8

Prep Time:
20 minutes

Pressure Cooking Time:
23 minutes

Release Method:
QUICK

Ingredients:

3 pounds flank steak, cut into ½-inch strips

Salt and pepper

1 tablespoon sesame oil

3 cloves garlic, minced

½ cup hoisin sauce

¼ cup water

¼ cup low-sodium soy sauce

¼ cup light brown sugar

2 teaspoons minced fresh ginger

1 teaspoon crushed red pepper flakes

2 tablespoons cornstarch mixed with ¼ cup water

1 red pepper, diced

6 green onions, sliced into 1-inch pieces

Directions:

1. Season beef with salt and pepper. Add oil to inner pot. Set COOKING TIME to 20 minutes and press START. Heat oil for about 5 minutes. Add beef and cook until browned, about 15 minutes. Press CANCEL.

2. Add garlic, hoisin, water, soy sauce, brown sugar, ginger, and red pepper flakes and stir to combine. Close and lock lid. Adjust pressure valve on top to AIRTIGHT, set COOKING TIME to 20 minutes, and press START.

3. When cooking cycle has finished, release pressure by carefully setting valve to EXHAUST on top of lid. Once all of pressure has released, turn lid, unlock, and open.

4. With the cooker's lid off, set COOKING TIME to 3 minutes and press START. Add cornstarch mixture, red pepper, and green onions and stir to combine. Cook until thickened.

TIP Any fresh sliced or chopped vegetables can be added in Step 4. Simply set cooking time to 5 minutes and add the vegetables. Cook for 4 minutes, then add the cornstarch mixture. Serve beef over white rice or Asian noodles.

Beef with Broccoli

Hoisin sauce and soy sauce (or tamari) combine with pungent spices to recreate this takeout favorite. Serve over brown rice for extra-nutty flavor and fiber.

Serves:
8

Prep Time:
15 minutes

Pressure Cooking Time:
15 minutes

Release Method:
QUICK

Ingredients:

2 pounds flank steak, cut into ½-inch strips

Salt and pepper

2 tablespoons vegetable oil

3 cloves garlic, minced

½ cup hoisin sauce

¼ cup water

¼ cup low-sodium soy sauce

¼ cup light brown sugar

2 teaspoons minced fresh ginger

1 teaspoon crushed red pepper flakes

1 pound broccoli florets

2 tablespoons cornstarch mixed with ¼ cup water

Directions:

1. Season beef with salt and pepper. Add oil to inner pot. Set COOKING TIME to 15 minutes and press START. Heat oil about 5 minutes. Add beef and cook until browned, about 10 minutes. Press CANCEL.

2. Add garlic, hoisin, water, soy sauce, brown sugar, ginger, and red pepper flakes and stir to combine. Close and lock lid. Adjust pressure valve on top to AIRTIGHT, set COOKING TIME to 15 minutes, and press START.

3. When cooking cycle has finished, release pressure by carefully setting valve to EXHAUST on top of lid. Once all of pressure has released, turn lid, unlock, and open.

4. With the cooker's lid off, set COOKING TIME to 5 minutes and press START. Add broccoli, stir, and cook until just softened, about 3 minutes. Add cornstarch mixture, stir, and cook until sauce thickens, about 2 minutes.

TIP Placing the flank steak in the freezer for 15 to 20 minutes prior to slicing will make it more firm and easier to slice.

Kicked Up Beef Ragu

Serves:
6 to 8

Prep Time:
25 minutes

Pressure Cooking Time:
25 minutes

Release Method:
QUICK

Ragu is typically slow cooked for hours at a very low temperature to develop deep, rich flavor. In the pressure cooker you get this rich flavor in less than an hour! It's great served with egg noodles or creamy polenta.

Ingredients:

1 tablespoon vegetable oil

5 slices bacon, chopped

2 pounds 95% lean ground beef

Salt and pepper

3 medium carrots, peeled, cut into 1-inch pieces

1 medium onion, chopped

1 green bell pepper, cut into 1-inch pieces

3 cloves garlic, minced

½ cup dry red wine

3 tablespoons tomato paste

2 teaspoons minced fresh thyme

1 pound medium white mushrooms, halved

1 medium zucchini, cut into 1-inch pieces

Directions:

1. Add oil to inner pot. Set COOKING TIME to 25 minutes and press START. Heat oil about 5 minutes. Add bacon and cook until browned, about 10 minutes. Transfer bacon to paper towel-lined plate. Set aside.

2. Season ground beef with salt and pepper. Add beef to pot and cook until browned, about 10 minutes. Press CANCEL.

3. Add carrots, onion, pepper, garlic, wine, tomato paste, and thyme and stir to combine. Close and lock lid. Adjust pressure valve on top to AIRTIGHT, set COOKING TIME to 20 minutes, and press START.

4. When cooking cycle has finished, release pressure by carefully setting valve to EXHAUST on top of lid. Once all of pressure has released, turn lid, unlock, and open.

5. With the cooker's lid off, set COOKING TIME to 5 minutes and press START. Add mushrooms and zucchini and stir to combine. Cook until vegetables are softened, about 5 minutes. Stir to combine, and serve.

TIP Serve this hearty ragu over egg noodles or your favorite cooked pasta.

Beef Ravioli with Marinara

Serves:
6 to 8

Prep Time:
5 minutes

Pressure Cooking Time:
4 minutes +
5 minute rest

Release Method:
QUICK

This is a perfect dish for those nights when you don't have much time to get dinner on the table. Just grab a bag of frozen ravioli and a jar of marinara sauce and toss it in the pot. No need to thaw! When the ravioli is ready, freshen the dish with some chopped parsley. Dinner is done in less than 10 minutes!

Ingredients:

1 (24 oz.) jar marinara

1 ⅔ cups water

1 ½ pounds frozen beef ravioli

1 tablespoon Italian seasoning, we recommend Great Flavors® Italian Seasoning

¼ cup minced fresh parsley

Directions:

1. Add all ingredients, in the order listed, except parsley, to inner pot and stir to combine, ensuring pasta is below water level. Close and lock lid. Adjust pressure valve on top to AIRTIGHT, set COOKING TIME to 4 minutes, and press START.

2. When cooking cycle has finished, release pressure by carefully setting valve to EXHAUST on top of lid. Once all of pressure has released, turn lid, unlock, and open.

3. Add parsley and stir to combine. Cover and let rest for 5 minutes before serving.

TIP Keep fresh herbs such as basil, oregano, tarragon, or thyme on hand for an easy way to add extra flavor to the dish.

One Pot Pasta & Meatballs

Serves:
6 to 8

Prep Time:
5 minutes

Pressure Cooking Time:
7 minutes +
5 minute rest

Release Method:
QUICK

Cooking the pasta, meatballs, and sauce together in one pot—no pasta draining required—means only one pot for cleanup. Quick and easy. Can't beat that!

Ingredients:

10 ounces medium shell pasta

1 pound frozen meatballs

2 ½ cups water

1 (24 oz.) jar marinara

1 tablespoon Italian seasoning, we recommend Great Flavors® Italian Seasoning

½ cup grated Parmesan cheese

Directions:

1. Add all ingredients, except Parmesan, to inner pot and stir to combine, ensuring pasta is below the water level. Close and lock lid. Adjust pressure valve on top to AIRTIGHT, set COOKING TIME to 7 minutes, and press START.

2. When cooking cycle has finished, release pressure by carefully setting valve to EXHAUST on top of lid. Once all of pressure has released, turn lid, unlock, and open.

3. Let rest, covered, for 5 minutes.

4. Transfer pasta to serving dish and sprinkle with Parmesan.

TIP If you want extra cheese-y pasta, add 1½ cups shredded mozzarella cheese in Step 3. The 5-minute rest time will melt the cheese perfectly.

Yankee Pot Roast

Serves:
10

Prep Time:
40 minutes

Pressure
Cooking Time:
70 minutes
(includes
pressure
release time)

Release Method:
NATURAL
AND QUICK

Yankee Pot Roast is is the one-pot meal filled with delicious beef, red potatoes, and a mélange of onions, carrots, and celery cooked in a rich, herbed wine and beef sauce. Serve with warm crusty bread to make this meal complete.

Ingredients:

4 pounds chuck roast, cut into 2-inch pieces

Salt and pepper

1 tablespoon vegetable oil

2 ½ cups beef broth, we recommend Great Flavors® Beef Stock Concentrate

¾ cup red wine

1 (6 oz.) can tomato paste

3 cloves garlic, minced

2 bay leaves

1 teaspoon dried thyme

10 small red potatoes, cut in half

3 stalks celery, cut into 1-inch pieces

2 medium onions, quartered

2 cups baby carrots

Directions:

1. Season beef with salt and pepper. Add oil to inner pot. Set COOKING TIME to 20 minutes and press START. Heat oil about 5 minutes. Add beef and cook until browned, about 15 minutes. Press CANCEL.

2. Add broth, red wine, tomato paste, garlic, bay leaves, and thyme and stir to combine. Close and lock lid. Adjust pressure valve on top to AIRTIGHT, set COOKING TIME to 40 minutes, and press START.

3. When cooking cycle has finished, let pressure drop NATURALLY. Once all of pressure has released, turn lid, unlock, and open.

4. Add potatoes, celery, onion, and carrots and stir to combine. Close and lock lid. Adjust pressure valve on top to AIRTIGHT, set COOKING TIME to 10 minutes, and press START.

5. When cooking cycle has finished, release pressure by carefully setting valve to EXHAUST on top of lid. Once all of pressure has released, turn lid, unlock, and open. Season with salt and pepper.

TIP Bottom round roast or brisket can be used instead of chuck roast.

Irish Beef Stew

Serves:
8 to 10

Prep Time:
15 minutes

Pressure Cooking Time:
1 hour
15 minutes
(includes pressure release time)

Release Method:
NATURAL
& QUICK

Cooking the beef in Irish stout adds robust, malty flavor to this stew. Carrots, potatoes, and onion are cooked at the end to ensure they are tender but not overcooked. Perfect for a St. Patrick's Day celebration!

Ingredients:

3 pounds chuck roast, cut into 2-inch pieces

Salt and pepper

1 tablespoon vegetable oil

1 (12 oz.) bottle dark Irish beer

½ cup beef broth, we recommend Great Flavors® Beef Stock Concentrate

3 cloves garlic, minced

3 tablespoons tomato paste

2 bay leaves

4 medium red potatoes, cubed

3 medium carrots, peeled, chopped

1 medium onion, chopped

3 tablespoons cornstarch mixed with ¼ cup water

Directions:

1. Season beef with salt and pepper. Add oil to inner pot. Set COOKING TIME to 15 minutes and press START. Heat oil about 5 minutes. Add beef and cook until browned, about 10 minutes. Press CANCEL.

2. Add beer, broth, garlic, tomato paste, and bay leaves and stir to combine. Close and lock lid. Adjust pressure valve on top to AIRTIGHT, set COOKING TIME to 40 minutes, and press START.

3. When cooking cycle has finished, let pressure drop NATURALLY. Once all of pressure has released, turn lid, unlock, and open.

4. Add potatoes, carrots, and onion. Close and lock lid. Adjust pressure valve on top to AIRTIGHT, set COOKING TIME to 15 minutes, and press START.

5. When cooking cycle has finished, release pressure by carefully setting valve to EXHAUST on top of lid. Once all of pressure has released, turn lid, unlock, and open.

6. With the cooker's lid off, set COOKING TIME to 2 minutes and press START. Add cornstarch mixture and stir to combine. Cook until thickened, about 2 minutes. Season with salt and pepper.

TIP To sop up all of the rich broth, serve with a biscuit, crusty bread, or in a bread bowl.

Chicago-Style Chili

Serves:
8 to 10

Prep Time:
15 minutes

Pressure Cooking Time:
15 minutes

Release Method:
QUICK

Chicago is famous for lots of amazing food—deep dish pizza, Chicago-style hot dogs, Italian Beef sandwiches—and now you can get to know this Chicago favorite. This ground beef chili is enhanced with a bottle of chili sauce that gives it a sweet and tangy flavor.

Ingredients:

2 ½ pounds 95% lean ground beef

Salt and pepper

1 tablespoon vegetable oil

2 medium onions, diced

4 cloves garlic, minced

1 green bell pepper, diced

1 (15 oz.) can tomato sauce

1 (14.5 oz.) can diced tomatoes

1 (12 oz.) bottle chili sauce

2 tablespoons chili powder

1 tablespoon dried oregano

1 teaspoon ground cumin

Directions:

1. Season beef with salt and pepper. Add oil to inner pot. Set COOKING TIME to 15 minutes and press START. Heat oil about 5 minutes. Add beef and cook until browned, about 10 minutes. Press CANCEL.

2. Add onion, garlic, pepper, tomato sauce, diced tomatoes, chili sauce, chili powder, oregano, and cumin and stir to combine. Close and lock lid. Adjust pressure valve on top to AIRTIGHT, set COOKING TIME to 15 minutes, and press START.

3. When cooking cycle has finished, release pressure by carefully setting valve to EXHAUST on top of lid. Once all of pressure has released, turn lid, unlock, and open.

TIP For Southwestern-style chili, add 1 can cooked and drained black beans and 1 can corn after pressure cooking. With cooker's lid off, set cooking time for 4 minutes and cook until heated through.

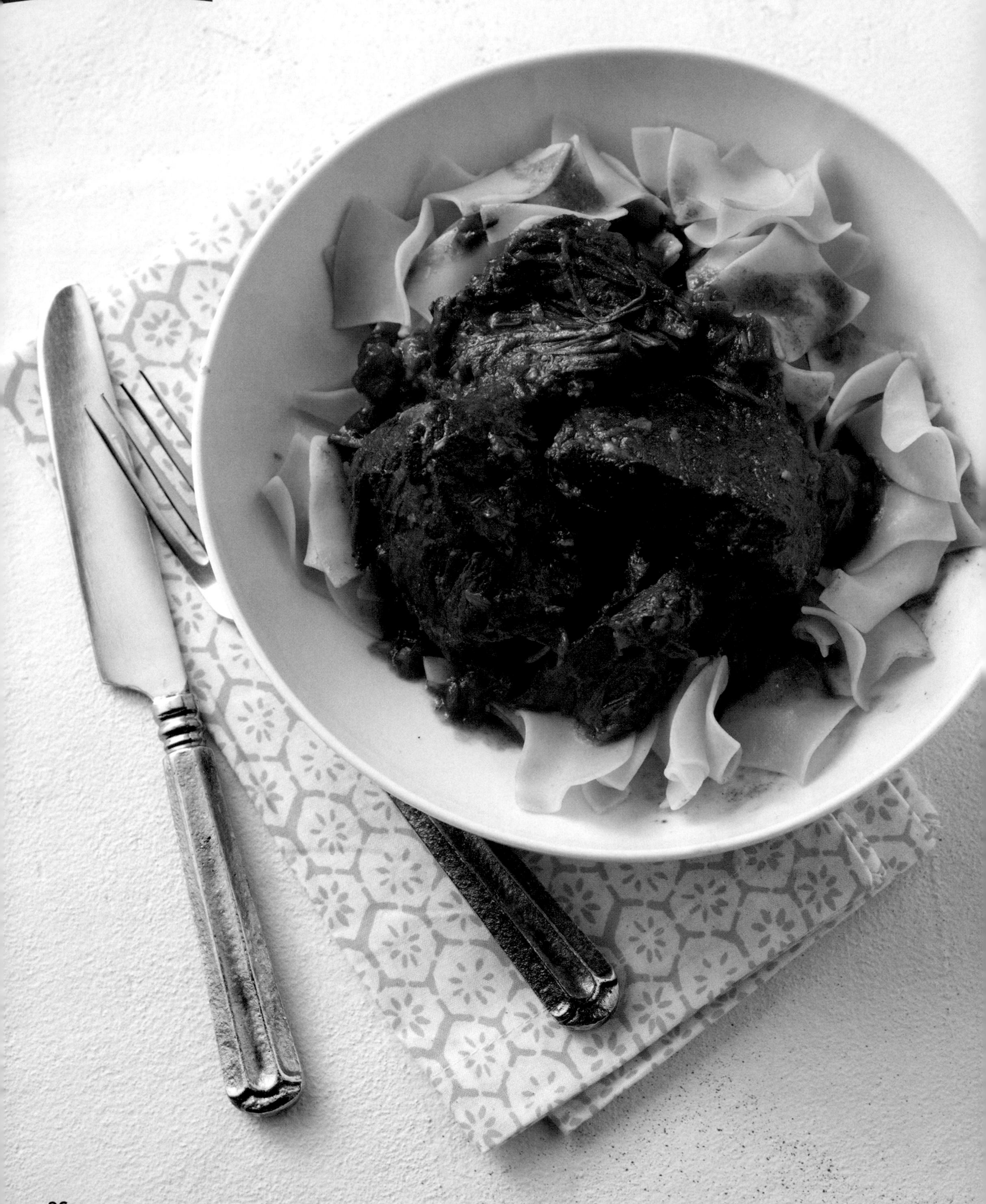

Braised Hungarian Short Ribs

Serves:
8

Prep Time:
20 minutes

Pressure Cooking Time:
1 hour
(includes pressure release time)

Release Method:
NATURAL

There's nothing better than hearty short ribs over mashed potatoes on a chilly evening. The smokiness of the paprika balances the rich beef gravy.

Ingredients:

1 tablespoon vegetable oil

4 pounds boneless beef short ribs

Salt and pepper

½ cup beef broth, we recommend Great Flavors® Beef Stock Concentrate

1 (8 oz.) can tomato sauce

1 medium onion, chopped

3 cloves garlic, minced

¼ cup light brown sugar

¼ cup apple cider vinegar

3 tablespoons Hungarian paprika

Directions:

1. Season short ribs with salt and pepper. Add oil to inner pot. Set COOKING TIME to 20 minutes and press START. Heat oil about 5 minutes. Add short ribs and cook until browned, about 15 minutes. Press CANCEL.

2. Add broth, tomato sauce, onion, garlic, brown sugar, vinegar, and paprika and stir to combine. Close and lock lid. Adjust pressure valve on top to AIRTIGHT, set COOKING TIME to 40 minutes, and press START.

3. When cooking cycle has finished, let pressure drop NATURALLY. Once all of pressure has released, turn lid, unlock, and open.

4. Remove short ribs. If you like a thicker sauce, mix 3 tablespoons cornstarch and a ¼ cup water in a small bowl. Set COOKING TIME to 2 minutes and press START. Add cornstarch mixture and stir to combine. Cook until thickened.

TIP For a smokier version, substitute smoked paprika in place of Hungarian paprika.

Serves:
8

Prep Time:
20 minutes

Pressure Cooking Time:
50 minutes (includes pressure release time)

Release Method:
NATURAL

Swiss Steak

The pressure cooker tenderizes the tough round steak in no time to create an amazing texture, while braising the meat in beef stock and tomato gravy infuses the meat with all of the wonderful flavor. Make sure to naturally release the pressure to keep all those delicious juices in the meat.

Ingredients:

3 pounds beef round, cut 1-inch pieces

Salt and pepper

1 tablespoon vegetable oil

½ cup beef broth, we recommend Great Flavors® Beef Stock Concentrate

1 medium onion, chopped

1 (14.5 oz.) can diced tomatoes, drained

3 tablespoons tomato paste

1 teaspoon dried oregano

2 tablespoons cornstarch mixed with ¼ cup water

Directions:

1. Season beef with salt and pepper. Add oil to inner pot. Set COOKING TIME to 20 minutes and press START. Heat oil about 5 minutes. Add beef and cook until browned, about 15 minutes. Press CANCEL.

2. Add broth, onion, tomatoes, tomato paste, and oregano, and stir to combine. Close and lock lid. Adjust pressure valve on top to AIRTIGHT, set COOKING TIME to 30 minutes, and press START.

3. When cooking cycle has finished, let pressure drop NATURALLY. Once all of pressure has released, turn lid, unlock, and open.

4. Set COOKING TIME to 3 minutes and press START. Add cornstarch mixture and stir to combine. Cook until thickened.

TIP For a complete meal, boil some egg noodles and serve beneath or alongside the steak and sauce.

Steak Au Poivre

Steak au Poivre, steak coated in crushed peppercorns, can sometimes be overwhelmingly peppery. Our recipe lets you decide how peppery you want it. We recommend that you add a modest amount of crushed peppercorns from a pepper grinder before you sauté the steak then add some at the end to get to the spiciness you desire.

Serves:
8

Prep Time:
20 minutes

Pressure Cooking Time:
45 minutes (includes pressure release time)

Release Method:
NATURAL

Ingredients:

3 pounds beef flank steak, cut into 2-inch pieces

Salt and pepper

1 tablespoon vegetable oil

1 medium onion, diced

1 cup red wine

½ cup heavy cream

2 tablespoons minced fresh rosemary

Directions:

1. Season with salt and pepper. Add oil to inner pot. Set COOKING TIME to 20 minutes and press START. Heat oil about 5 minutes. Add beef and cook until browned, about 15 minutes. Press CANCEL.

2. Add onion, red wine, heavy cream, and rosemary and stir to combine. Close and lock lid. Adjust pressure valve on top to AIRTIGHT, set COOKING TIME to 25 minutes, and press START.

3. When cooking cycle has finished, let pressure drop NATURALLY. Once all of pressure has released, turn lid, unlock, and open. Season with salt and pepper.

TIP This steak is typically coated in a crust of crushed black peppercorns. Depending on how pungent you like it, add more pepper to your taste.

Corned Beef with Dijon

The spicy Dijon and sweet brown sugar add a new twist on classic corned beef in this delicious recipe. Serve with braised cabbage or herbed potatoes, then slice the leftovers for corned beef sandwiches the next day.

Serves:
8

Prep Time:
5 minutes

Pressure Cooking Time:
1 hour
15 minutes
(includes pressure release time)

Release Method:
NATURAL

Ingredients:

1 (3 ½ to 4 lb.) corned beef

1 medium onion, sliced thin

1½ cups water

¾ cup Dijon mustard

¼ cup light brown sugar

2 teaspoons black pepper

½ teaspoon ground cloves

Directions:

1. Add all ingredients to inner pot. Close and lock lid. Adjust pressure valve on top to AIRTIGHT, set COOKING TIME to 55 minutes, and press START.

2. When cooking cycle has finished, let pressure drop NATURALLY. Once all of pressure has released, turn lid, unlock, and open.

3. Transfer corned beef to a cutting board, let rest for 10 minutes, then slice. Drizzle corned beef with cooking liquid before serving.

TIP When purchasing the corned beef, buy a point cut or one that is more round. These will have more marbling, which equals more flavor.

Philly Cheesesteak

Serves:
8

Prep Time:
20 minutes

Pressure Cooking Time:
55 minutes (includes pressure release time)

Release Method:
NATURAL

Browning the steak with the steak seasoning before pressure cooking it in rich beef broth provides the best in texture and flavor. Using provolone cheese, melted on top, makes this cheesesteak truly authentic.

Ingredients:

4 pounds flank steak, cut into ¼-inch strips

2 tablespoons steak seasoning

1 tablespoon vegetable oil

¼ cup beef broth, we recommend Great Flavors® Beef Stock Concentrate

2 medium onions, sliced thin

½ pound sliced provolone cheese

8 sub or hoagie rolls

Directions:

1. Season beef with steak seasoning. Add oil to inner pot. Set COOKING TIME to 20 minutes and press START. Heat oil about 5 minutes. Add beef and cook until browned, about 15 minutes. Press CANCEL.

2. Add broth and onions and stir to combine. Close and lock lid. Adjust pressure valve on top to AIRTIGHT, set COOKING TIME to 30 minutes, and press START.

3. When cooking cycle has finished, let pressure drop NATURALLY. Once all of pressure has released, turn lid, unlock, and open.

4. Drain cooking liquid. Add provolone cheese. Let rest, covered, for 5 minutes or until cheese is melted.

TIP For a truly authentic cheesesteak, use Amaroso rolls if you can find them in your market. This is the roll used in Philadelphia and the surrounding area. If you can't find that brand, use a roll that is not overly crusty outside and fluffy inside.

PORK

Italian Sausage with Ziti & Red Sauce, 94

Serves:
10

Prep Time:
15 minutes

Pressure Cooking Time:
8 minutes +
5 minute rest

Release Method:
QUICK

Italian Sausage with Ziti & Red Sauce

Ziti rigati, with its ridges and hollow center, is the perfect foil for our flavorful marinara sauce. Take a trip to Italy with every bite. This tasty dish is ready in less than 30 minutes.

Ingredients:

1 tablespoon vegetable oil

2 pounds Italian sausage, cut into 1-inch rounds

10 ounces ziti

2 ¾ cups water

1 (24 oz.) jar marinara

1 tablespoon Italian seasoning, we recommend Great Flavors® Italian Seasoning

½ cup grated Parmesan cheese

Directions:

1. Add oil to inner pot. Set COOKING TIME to 15 minutes, and press START. Heat oil about 5 minutes. Add Italian sausage and cook until browned, about 10 minutes. Press CANCEL.

2. Add ziti, water, marinara, and Italian seasoning and stir to combine, ensuring pasta is below the water level. Close and lock lid. Adjust pressure valve on top to AIRTIGHT, set COOKING TIME to 8 minutes, and press START.

3. When cooking cycle has finished, release pressure by carefully setting valve to EXHAUST on top of lid. Once all of pressure has released, turn lid, unlock, and open.

4. Let pasta sit in pressure cooker with lid closed for 5 minutes. Transfer pasta to serving dish and sprinkle with Parmesan.

TIP Adding a couple dollops of ricotta cheese in step 4 will add a creamy texture and slightly sweet flavor.

Kielbasa with Brussels Kraut

Shaved brussels sprouts are combined with traditional kraut ingredients to create a great spin on traditional sauerkraut. The sharp, tangy kraut is perfect to offset the rich, smokiness of the Kielbasa.

Serves:
10

Prep Time:
15 minutes

Pressure Cooking Time:
8 minutes

Release Method:
QUICK

Ingredients:

1 tablespoon vegetable oil

2 pounds kielbasa sausage, cut into 1-inch rounds

1 medium onion, sliced thin

1 pound Brussel sprouts, shaved thin

½ cup chicken broth, we recommend Great Flavors® Chicken Stock Concentrate

⅓ cup ketchup

¼ cup apple cider vinegar

2 tablespoons light brown sugar

1 teaspoon caraway seeds

3 cloves garlic, minced

Salt and pepper

Directions:

1. Add oil to inner pot. Set COOKING TIME to 15 minutes and press START. Heat oil about 5 minutes. Add kielbasa and cook until browned, about 10 minutes. Press CANCEL.

2. Add onion, Brussel sprouts, broth, ketchup, vinegar, brown sugar, caraway seeds and garlic and stir to combine. Season with salt and pepper. Close and lock lid. Adjust pressure valve on top to AIRTIGHT, set COOKING TIME to 8 minutes, and press START.

3. When cooking cycle has finished, release pressure by carefully setting valve to EXHAUST on top of lid. Once all of pressure has released, turn lid, unlock, and open.

TIP Unable to find Brussel sprouts or you just don't like them? Substitute green cabbage or canned sauerkraut in its place.

Kansas City Ribs

Serves:
8

Prep Time:
20 minutes

Pressure Cooking Time:
50 minutes
(includes pressure release time)

Release Method:
NATURAL

These finger-lickin' favorites can have the perfect balance of sweet, smoky, and spicy every time. Just choose your favorite barbeque sauce. Add variety with different sauces from meal to meal. Whatever you do, be sure to have plenty of napkins on hand.

Ingredients:

½ **cup light brown sugar**

2 tablespoons smoked paprika

1 teaspoon garlic powder

1 teaspoon onion powder

Salt and pepper

2 racks baby back ribs, cut to fit into cooker

½ **cup beef broth, we recommend Great Flavors® Beef Stock Concentrate**

1 (18 oz.) bottle barbecue sauce

Directions:

1. In a small bowl combine brown sugar, paprika, garlic powder, and onion powder. Season with salt and pepper.

2. Season ribs with spice rub and place in inner pot. Add broth and barbecue sauce. Close and lock lid. Adjust pressure valve on top to AIRTIGHT, set COOKING TIME to 30 minutes, and press START.

3. When cooking cycle has finished, let pressure drop NATURALLY. Once all of pressure has released, turn lid, unlock, and open.

TIP To make it easier to cut the ribs, turn them on their side. You can see the meat between the bones and cut into portions quickly.

Serves:
12 to 14

Prep Time:
20 minutes

**Pressure
Cooking Time:**
1 hour 5 minutes
(includes
pressure
release time)

Release Method:
NATURAL

Spicy Sriracha Pulled Pork

Pulled pork usually needs to cook all day in an oven or on a grill, but you can pressure cook this pork shoulder for only an hour and it will be pull-apart tender. The shredded pork is ready for sliders or sandwiches in no time. The Sriracha spices it up!

Ingredients:

5 to 5½ pounds pork shoulder or butt, cut into 4 inch-pieces

Salt and pepper

1 tablespoon vegetable oil

½ cup chicken broth, we recommend Great Flavors® Chicken Stock Concentrate

¼ cup rice vinegar

1 (8 oz.) can tomato sauce

⅓ cup Sriracha sauce

2 tablespoons light brown sugar

1 tablespoon chili powder

1 tablespoon paprika

1 tablespoon minced fresh ginger

Directions:

1. Season pork with salt and pepper. Add oil to inner pot. Set COOKING TIME to 20 minutes and press START. Heat oil about 5 minutes. Add pork and cook until browned, about 15 minutes. Press CANCEL.

2. Add broth, vinegar, tomato sauce, Sriracha, brown sugar, chili powder, paprika, and ginger and stir to combine. Close and lock lid. Adjust pressure valve on top to AIRTIGHT, set COOKING TIME to 45 minutes, and press START.

3. When cooking cycle has finished, let pressure drop NATURALLY. Once all of pressure has released, turn lid, unlock, and open.

4. Transfer pork to a large bowl and shred with two forks. Add some cooking liquid to shredded pork until moistened.

TIP For smokiness, add 1 teaspoon liquid smoke in Step 2.

Pork Cassoulet

Serves:
10

Prep Time:
35 minutes +
beans soaked
overnight

**Pressure
Cooking Time:**
30 minutes

Release Method:
QUICK

This recipe probably has the most ingredients of any recipe in this book. Yet each ingredient makes an important contribution to the complex flavors of this classic French dish. Normally, cassoulet is cooked all day; this version takes only 30 minutes in the pressure cooker.

Ingredients:

½ **pound dried Great Northern beans**

1 **tablespoon vegetable oil**

½ **pound bacon, cut into 2-inch pieces**

2 **pounds country-style pork spareribs, cut into 2-inch pieces**

Salt and pepper

½ **pound smoked sausage, cut into 1-inch rounds**

1 **medium onion, chopped**

1 **cup chicken broth, we recommend Great Flavors® Chicken Stock Concentrate**

1 **(14.5 oz.) can diced tomatoes, drained**

¼ **cup tomato paste**

4 **cloves garlic, minced**

1 **teaspoon fennel seeds**

2 **bay leaves**

3 **cups French bread, cut into 1-inch pieces**

Directions:

1. In a large bowl, cover beans with at least 3 inches of water. Refrigerate and soak overnight. Drain and rinse beans and set aside.

2. Add oil to inner pot. Set COOKING TIME to 25 minutes and press START. Heat oil about 5 minutes. Add bacon and cook until browned, about 10 minutes. Remove bacon and set aside.

3. Add spareribs to pot. Cook until browned, about 10 minutes. Press CANCEL.

4. Add reserved cooked bacon, sausage, onion, broth, tomatoes, tomato paste, garlic, fennel seeds, and and bay leaves. Season with salt and pepper. Close and lock lid. Adjust pressure valve on top to AIRTIGHT, set COOKING TIME to 30 minutes, and press START.

5. When cooking cycle has finished, release pressure by carefully setting valve to EXHAUST on top of lid. Once all of pressure has released, turn lid, unlock, and open.

6. Top pork with French bread and serve.

TIP Bone-in, skinless, chicken thighs or skinless duck legs can be substituted for the pork.

Pork Roast with Sage Gravy

Serves:
8 to 10

Prep Time:
15 minutes

Pressure
Cooking Time:
1 hour, 10 minutes
(includes
pressure
release time)

Release Method:
NATURAL

In the pressure cooker, the roast will actually reabsorb its own juices and the sage will season the entire juicy roast. The gravy is especially wonderful, and is a perfect addition to mashed potatoes.

Ingredients:

4 to 4 ½ pounds pork shoulder or butt

Salt and pepper

1 tablespoon vegetable oil

½ cup chicken broth, we recommend Great Flavors® Chicken Stock Concentrate

1 medium onion, chopped

2 tablespoons Dijon mustard

2 tablespoons fresh minced sage

4 cloves garlic, sliced

3 tablespoons cornstarch mixed with ¼ cup milk

2 tablespoons unsalted butter

Directions:

1. Season pork with salt and pepper. Add oil to inner pot. Set COOKING TIME to 15 minutes and press START. Heat oil about 5 minutes. Add pork and cook ntil browned, about 10 minutes. Press CANCEL.

2. Add broth, onion, mustard, sage, and garlic and stir to combine. Close and lock lid. Adjust pressure valve on top to AIRTIGHT, set COOKING TIME to 45 minutes, press START.

3. When cooking cycle has finished, let pressure drop NATURALLY. Once all of pressure has released, turn lid, unlock, and open.

4. Remove pork, and let rest, covered with aluminum foil before carving and serving.

5. Set COOKING TIME to 4 minutes and press START. Add cornstarch mixture and butter and stir to combine. Cook until sauce thickens.

TIP Substituting apple cider in place of the broth will add a new depth of flavor to this dish.

Five Spice Pork Chops

Serves:
8

Prep Time:
15 minutes

Pressure Cooking Time:
10 minutes

Release Method:
QUICK

If you haven't yet tried five-spice powder (star anise, cloves, Chinese cinnamon, Sichuan pepper and fennel seeds), try this tasty recipe with this tried-and-true Asian combination of spices. This flavorful dish will have your guests begging for the recipe.

Ingredients:

8 (4 oz.) boneless, thick-cut pork chops

Salt and pepper

1 tablespoon vegetable oil

½ cup chicken broth, we recommend Great Flavors® Chicken Stock Concentrate

3 tablespoons soy sauce

2 teaspoons five spice powder

1 teaspoon minced fresh ginger

Directions:

1. Season pork with salt and pepper. Add oil to inner pot. Set COOKING TIME to 15 minutes and press START. Heat oil about 5 minutes. Add pork and cook until browned, about 10 minutes. Press CANCEL.

2. Add broth, soy sauce, five spice powder, and ginger and stir to combine. Close and lock lid. Adjust pressure valve on top to AIRTIGHT, set COOKING TIME to 10 minutes, and press START.

3. When cooking cycle has finished, release pressure by carefully setting valve to EXHAUST on top of lid. Once all of pressure has released, turn lid, unlock, and open.

TIP Five spice powder can be found in the Asian section of the supermarket. You can make your own by combining equal parts ground cinnamon, ground cloves, fennel seeds, star anise and Sichuan peppercorns and grinding to a powder in a spice grinder.

Apple Pie Pork Chops

Serves:
8

Prep Time:
30 minutes

Pressure Cooking Time:
12 minutes

Release Method:
QUICK

This a festive approach to pork chops crunchy cranberry/apple topping, reminiscent of Christmas baking, makes this a perfect meal any time during the holiday season.

Ingredients:

1 (9 oz.) box pie crust mix

8 (4 oz.) boneless pork chops

Salt and pepper

2 tablespoons vegetable oil

2 apples, peeled, seeded, and chopped

½ cup apple cider

¼ cup light brown sugar

¼ cup sweetened dried cranberries

½ teaspoon ground ginger

¼ teaspoon cinnamon

1 teaspoon cornstarch mixed with 2 tablespoons water

Directions:

1. Follow directions on pie crust mix for making a half recipe pie crust. Bake, crumble into large pieces, and set aside.

2. Season pork with salt and pepper. Add oil to inner pot. Set COOKING TIME to 15 minutes and press START. Heat oil about 5 minutes. Add pork and cook until browned, about 10 minutes. Press CANCEL.

3. Add apples, cider, brown sugar, cranberries, ginger, and cinnamon and stir to combine. Close and lock lid. Adjust pressure valve on top to AIRTIGHT, set COOKING TIME to 10 minutes, and press START.

4. When cooking cycle has finished, release pressure by carefully setting valve to EXHAUST on top of lid. Once all pressure has released, turn lid, unlock, and open.

5. Remove pork and let rest, covered with aluminum foil, for 5 minutes.

6. Set COOKING TIME to 2 minutes and press START. Add cornstarch mixture to apple gravy and stir combine. Cook until thickened. Serve pork chops topped with apple gravy and pie crumbles.

TIP When buying pork chops, look in the specialty section of your butcher shop for Berkshire or Duroc pork. This pork will be juicier, more tender, and have a robust flavor.

Cranberry Pork Tenderloin

Serves:
10

Prep Time:
15 minutes

Pressure Cooking Time:
23 minutes

Release Method:
QUICK

This loin will be tender, indeed, thanks to the power of pressure-cooking. The process also helps the roast soak up the delightful combination of cranberries, cloves, brown sugar and vinegar.

Ingredients:

3 (1 to 1 ½ lbs.) pork tenderloins

Salt and pepper

1 tablespoon vegetable oil

1 cup frozen cranberries

¼ cup orange juice

3 tablespoons light brown sugar

2 tablespoons balsamic vinegar

¼ teaspoon ground cloves

2 tablespoons cornstarch mixed with ¼ cup water

Directions:

1. Season pork with salt and pepper. Add oil to inner pot. Set COOKING TIME to 15 minutes and press START. Heat oil about 5 minutes. Add pork and cook until browned, about 10 minutes. Press CANCEL.

2. Add cranberries, orange juice, brown sugar, balsamic vinegar, and cloves and stir to combine. Close and lock lid. Adjust pressure valve on top to AIRTIGHT, set COOKING TIME to 20 minutes, and press START.

3. When cooking cycle has finished, release pressure by carefully setting valve to EXHAUST on top of lid. Once all of pressure has released, turn lid, unlock, and open.

4. Remove pork and let rest, covered with aluminum foil, for 5 minutes before carving and serving.

5. Set COOKING TIME to 3 minutes and press START. Add cornstarch mixture and stir to combine. Cook until sauce thickens.

TIP A great way to enhance the flavor is by marinating the pork. The marinade can be simply garlic and oil or a store bought vinaigrette. Marinate the pork in a storage container overnight. Drain marinade and pat pork dry prior to Step 1.

Shredded Pork Street Tacos

Serves:
12 to 14

Prep Time:
10 minutes

Pressure Cooking Time:
1 hour
(includes pressure release time)

Release Method:
NATURAL

This recipe is a version of pulled pork, but with chili powder, cumin, coriander and garlic to give it Mexican street taco flair. Muy bueno!

Ingredients:

5 to 5½ pounds pork shoulder or butt, cut into 4 inch-pieces

2 tablespoons light brown sugar

1 tablespoon chili powder

1 tablespoon ground cumin

1 tablespoon ground coriander

1 teaspoon garlic powder

1 teaspoon dried oregano

1 cup chicken broth, we recommend Great Flavors® Chicken Stock Concentrate

Salt and pepper

½ cup orange juice

SERVE WITH:

Warm corn or flour

Giardiniera vegetables, chopped

Directions:

1. Add all ingredients to inner pot. Close and lock lid. Adjust pressure valve on top to AIRTIGHT, set COOKING TIME to 45 minutes, and press START.

2. When cooking cycle has finished, let pressure drop NATURALLY. Once all of pressure has released, turn lid, unlock, and open.

3. Transfer pork to a large bowl and shred with two forks. Add some cooking liquid back to shredded pork to moisten. Season with salt and pepper.

4. Serve with warm corn or flour tortillas and chopped giardiniera vegetables.

TIP To make this dish truly authentic, add some shredded Queso Fresco, fresh Mexican cheese, to your tacos.

Serves:
10

Prep Time:
15 minutes

**Pressure
Cooking Time:**
7 minutes

Release Method:
QUICK

Tater Tot Casserole with Ham

This is not a diet dish This is pure indulgence. But the combination of cheese, ham, and tater tots brimming with mushroom flavor is irresistible.

Ingredients:

1 cup chicken broth, we recommend Great Flavors® Chicken Stock Concentrate

1 (32 oz.) bag frozen tater tots

1 ½ pounds boneless ham, diced

2 green bell peppers, seeded, diced

1 medium onion, diced

2 ½ cups shredded cheddar cheese

1 (10.5 oz.) can cream of mushroom soup

Directions:

1. Place broth into inner pot. Add half of tater tots, then half of ham, half of peppers, half of onion, and half of cheese. Repeat layering with remaining ingredients. Top with soup.

2. Close and lock lid. Adjust pressure valve on top to AIRTIGHT, set COOKING TIME to 7 minutes, and press START.

3. When cooking cycle has finished, release pressure by carefully setting valve to EXHAUST on the top of lid. Once all of pressure has released, turn lid, unlock, and open.

TIP This recipe can be made using different meats or vegetables. In place of the ham, cook 2 pounds ground beef or turkey in the pressure cooker then start with Step 1.

FISH

Bayou Bouilibaisse, 117

Serves:
8

Prep Time:
10 minutes

Pressure Cooking Time:
6 minutes

Release Method:
QUICK

Mediterranean Sword Fish

The sharp, tanginess of sun-dried tomatoes, olives, and roasted red peppers are a perfect match for this meaty fish. You will be quickly transported to a seaside Mediterranean village when you pop open the lid.

Ingredients:

8 (4 oz.) swordfish fillets

⅓ cup sundried tomatoes, chopped

¼ cup chicken broth, we recommend Great Flavors® Chicken Stock Concentrate

¼ cup roasted red peppers, chopped

¼ cup store-bought olive tapenade

2 tablespoons extra-virgin olive oil

1 tablespoon minced fresh oregano

1 tablespoon minced fresh ginger

Directions:

1. Add all ingredients to inner pot. Close and lock lid. Adjust pressure valve on top to AIRTIGHT, set COOKING TIME to 6 minutes, and press START.

2. When cooking cycle has finished, release pressure by carefully setting valve to EXHAUST on top of lid. Once all of pressure has released, turn lid, unlock, and open.

3. Remove fish and pour sauce over the top.

Coconut Fish Curry

Serves:
6 to 8

Prep Time:
10 minutes

Pressure Cooking Time:
5 minutes

Release Method:
QUICK

From your world voyages with Mediterranean Swordfish and Teriyaki Tuna, you head to India with this Coconut Fish Curry. Mild, flaky cod is the perfect vehicle to soak up the bold flavors of the curry-infused coconut sauce.

Ingredients:

2 pounds cod fillets

Salt and pepper

½ cup unsweetened coconut milk

1 tomato, seeded and chopped

1 green bell pepper, seeded and chopped

1 tablespoon curry powder

¼ cup minced fresh cilantro

Directions:

1. Add cod, coconut milk, tomato, green pepper, and curry to inner pot. Season with salt and pepper. Close and lock lid. Adjust pressure valve on top to AIRTIGHT, set COOKING TIME to 5 minutes, and press START.

2. When cooking cycle has finished, release pressure by carefully setting valve to EXHAUST on top of lid. Once all of pressure has released, turn lid, unlock, and open.

3. Sprinkle cilantro on top and transfer fish to individual serving bowls. Pour coconut broth over fish.

TIP For a spicier broth, add 1 chopped serrano chili with the pepper in Step 1.

 # Teriyaki Tuna

The ginger, spices, and soy sauce will carry your taste buds all the way to Asia. Four minutes from start to finish is just the right amount of time to cook and season the tuna.

Serves:
8

Prep Time:
10 minutes

Pressure Cooking Time:
4 minutes

Release Method:
QUICK

Ingredients:

1 tablespoon extra-virgin olive oil

8 (4 oz.) tuna fillets

⅓ cup teriyaki sauce

3 tablespoons water

3 cloves garlic, minced

2 teaspoons fresh minced ginger

⅓ chopped green onions

1 tablespoon sesame seeds

Directions:

1. Add all ingredients in the order listed to inner pot, except green onions and sesame seeds. Close and lock lid. Adjust pressure valve on top to AIRTIGHT, set COOKING TIME to 4 minutes, and press START.

2. When cooking cycle has finished, release pressure by carefully setting valve to EXHAUST on top of lid. Once all of pressure has released, turn lid, unlock, and open.

3. Transfer tuna and sauce to serving dish. Sprinkle with green onions and sesame seeds.

TIP Any firm fish, such as swordfish, salmon or mahi-mahi, will work in this recipe.

Honey Mustard Salmon

Serves:
8

Prep Time:
10 minutes

Pressure Cooking Time:
5 minutes

Release Method:
QUICK

The sweet and spicy sauce makes this dinner a simple but yummy meal. From start to finish to your dinner table, this tasty salmon takes only 15 minutes. What could be easier?

Ingredients:

8 (4 oz.) salmon fillets

Salt and pepper

3 tablespoons lemon juice

¼ cup white wine

¼ cup Dijon mustard

¼ cup honey

2 tablespoons minced fresh dill

Directions:

1. Add salmon, lemon juice and white wine to inner pot. Season with salt and pepper.

2. Close and lock lid. Adjust pressure valve on top to AIRTIGHT, set COOKING TIME to 5 minutes, and press START.

3. When cooking cycle has finished, release pressure by carefully setting valve to EXHAUST on top of lid. Once all of pressure has released, turn lid, unlock, and open.

4. In a small bowl, combine mustard, honey and dill. Remove salmon and evenly spread mustard sauce on top of each fillet.

TIP This pressure-cooked salmon, with or without the sauce, can be added to pasta, a salad, or made into a sandwich.

Bayou Bouilibaisse

Bouillabaisse is a traditional French stew from the port city of Marseille. Bouillabaisse literally means to boil and simmer. Now you can do that whole job of simmering and infusing the flavors in just four minutes under pressure.

Serves:
6 to 8

Prep Time:
15 minutes

Pressure Cooking Time:
4 minutes

Release Method:
QUICK

Ingredients:

1 pound fresh mussels, cleaned and debearded

1 pound large shrimp, peeled and deveined

½ pound fresh cod, cut into 3-inch pieces

1 medium onion, chopped

½ bulb fennel, chopped

1 (8 oz.) can tomato sauce

1 (10.5 oz.) can clam juice

3 cloves garlic, minced

1 tablespoon Bayou Cajun seasoning

1 teaspoon minced fresh thyme

Directions:

1. Add all ingredients to inner pot. Close and lock lid. Adjust pressure valve on top to AIRTIGHT, set COOKING TIME to 4 minutes, and press START.

2. When cooking cycle has finished, release pressure by carefully setting valve to EXHAUST on top of lid. Once all of pressure has released, turn lid, unlock, and open. Transfer fish and broth to individual serving bowls.

TIP An equal weight of any seafood combination will work in this recipe.

Prep Time:
10 minutes

Pressure Cooking Time:
4 minutes

Release Method:
QUICK

Perfect Steamed Mussels

With fresh mussels available at most supermarkets, you can make this bistro favorite easily and quickly at home in the pressure cooker. Steam the mussels in broth enhanced with garlic, thyme, lemon, and red pepper flakes. Use crusty bread to sop up this delicious briny broth.

Ingredients:

2 pounds fresh mussels, cleaned and debearded

1 medium onion, chopped

3 tablespoons lemon juice

½ cup vegetable broth, we recommend Great Flavors® Vegetable Stock Concentrate

2 tablespoons unsalted butter

4 cloves garlic, minced

1 teaspoon minced fresh thyme

½ teaspoon crushed red pepper flakes

Directions:

1. Add all ingredients to inner pot. Close and lock lid. Adjust pressure valve on top to AIRTIGHT, set COOKING TIME to 4 minutes, and press START.

2. When cooking cycle has finished, release pressure by carefully setting valve to EXHAUST on top of lid. Once all of pressure has released, turn lid, unlock, and open. Discard any unopened mussels. Transfer mussels and broth mixture to individual serving bowls.

TIP You can substitute fresh littleneck or cherrystone clams for the mussels or cook a combination of mussels and clams. Don't forget a big loaf of crusty bread to soak up all of the wonderful broth.

PASTA, RICE & GRAINS

Lasagna Florentine, 120

Serves:
10

Prep Time:
15 minutes

**Pressure
Cooking Time:**
15 minutes +
10 minute rest

Release Method:
QUICK

Lasagna Florentine

Lasagna in 30 minutes? You've got that right. Creamy, cheesy spinach lasagna is flavored with a white Alfredo sauce and rich ricotta. Serve with a sliced tomato and basil salad for perfect balance.

Ingredients:

2 pounds ricotta cheese

2 pounds frozen chopped spinach, thawed

2 large eggs

½ cup grated Parmesan cheese

1 tablespoon Italian seasoning, we recommend Great Flavors® Italian Seasoning

Salt and pepper

1 ½ cups water, divided

2 (15 oz.) jars Alfredo sauce, divided

16 no-boil lasagna noodles, broken into ⅓, divided

2 cups shredded mozzarella cheese

Directions:

1. In a large bowl, combine ricotta cheese, spinach, eggs, Parmesan cheese and Italian seasoning. Season with salt and pepper.

2. Add ½ cup water and 1 jar Alfredo sauce to inner pot. Top with a ¼ of lasagna noodles then top noodles with ⅓ of the ricotta mixture.

3. Add ¼ more lasagna noodles, ½ cup water, ⅓ ricotta mixture, and ½ jar Alfredo sauce. Repeat with another layer of noodles, remaining ½ cup water, remaining ⅓ ricotta mixture, and remaining noodles. Top with remaining ½ jar Alfredo sauce.

4. Close and lock lid. Adjust pressure valve on top to AIRTIGHT, set COOKING TIME to 15 minutes, and press START.

5. When cooking cycle has finished, release pressure by carefully setting valve to EXHAUST on top of lid. Once all of pressure has released, turn lid, unlock, and open.

6. Add mozzarella cheese. Re-cover and let rest for 10 minutes before serving.

Campanelle Pasta Alfredo

What's the biggest problem with pasta Alfredo? The noodles just can't hold onto the rich, creamy sauce—it slides off into the bowl and you're searching for flavor. You won't have that problem with this recipe. The pasta is cooked in the sauce so it's got that great creamy texture and flavor.

Serves:
6 to 8

Prep Time:
5 minutes

**Pressure
Cooking Time:**
7 minutes +
5 minute rest

Release Method:
QUICK

Ingredients:

1 (15 oz.) jar Alfredo sauce

3 cups water

10 ounces campanelle pasta

⅓ cup grated Parmesan cheese

1 pint grape tomatoes, halved

½ cup chopped fresh basil

Salt and pepper

Directions:

1. Add Alfredo sauce, water, and pasta to inner pot and stir to combine, ensuring pasta is below the water level. Close and lock lid. Adjust pressure valve on top to AIRTIGHT, set COOKING TIME to 7 minutes, and press START.

2. When cooking cycle has finished, release pressure by carefully setting valve to EXHAUST on top of lid. Once all of pressure has released, turn lid, unlock, and open.

3. Add Parmesan, tomatoes, and basil. Season with salt and pepper and stir to combine. Let rest for 5 minutes before serving.

TIP When creating a pasta dish, remember, less is more. Limit the number of ingredients and be creative.

Shrimp Scampi with Bow Tie Pasta

In only 20 minutes you can have a meal that will make any weeknight special. The pasta is cooked in water seasoned with wine and garlic—no need to drain—making it both flavorful and easy. Adding the shrimp at the end avoids overcooking.

Serves:
8

Prep Time:
10 minutes

Pressure Cooking Time:
9 minutes

Release Method:
QUICK

Ingredients:

3 tablespoons extra-virgin olive oil

2 ¾ cups water

½ cup white wine

10 ounces bowtie pasta

4 cloves garlic, minced

Salt and pepper

1 pound large shrimp, peeled and deveined

2 tablespoons lemon juice

¼ cup chopped fresh parsley

3 tablespoons unsalted butter

Directions:

1. Add oil, water, wine, pasta, and garlic to inner pot. Season with salt and pepper. Stir to combine ingredients, ensuring pasta is below the water level.

2. Close and lock lid. Adjust pressure valve on top to AIRTIGHT, set COOKING TIME to 5 minutes, and press START.

3. When cooking cycle has finished, release pressure by carefully setting valve to EXHAUST on top of lid. Once all of pressure has released, turn lid, unlock, and open.

4. Add shrimp, lemon juice, parsley, and butter and stir to combine. Set COOKING TIME to 4 minutes and press START.

TIP For a nice kick, add ¾ teaspoon crushed red pepper flakes in Step 1.

Spinach Ravioli with Vodka Sauce

Serves:
8

Prep Time:
5 minutes

Pressure Cooking Time:
4 minutes +
5 minute rest

Release Method:
QUICK

Vodka sauce takes a typical tomato sauce up a notch by adding bite from vodka and richness from cream. You can easily find Vodka Sauce in the jarred tomato sauce aisle. Add it to frozen ravioli and you have a delicious meal without much work. Serve with your favorite tossed salad.

Ingredients:

1 (24 oz.) jar vodka pasta sauce

1 ⅔ cups water

1 ½ pounds frozen spinach ravioli

2 tablespoon Italian seasoning, we recommend Great Flavors® Italian Seasoning

¼ cup chopped fresh basil

Directions:

1. Add all ingredients in the order listed, except basil, to inner pot. Stir to combine, ensuring pasta is below the water level. Close and lock lid. Adjust pressure valve on top to AIRTIGHT, set COOKING TIME to 4 minutes, and press START.

2. When cooking cycle has finished, release pressure by carefully setting valve to EXHAUST on top of lid. Once all of pressure has released, turn lid, unlock, and open.

3. Add basil and season with salt and pepper. Stir to combine. Re-cover and let rest for 5 minutes before serving.

TIP Double the recipe and freeze extra servings for later.

Mac & Cheese

Serves:
6 to 8

Prep Time:
5 minutes

Pressure
Cooking Time:
12 minutes

Release Method:
QUICK

This homemade mac and cheese is almost as quick to make as that kind that comes in the little blue box. The pasta cooks right in the sauce—all you have to do is add the cheese and a little milk at the end. How easy is that?

Ingredients:

2 ½ cups whole milk, divided

1 ¼ cups water

10 ounces elbow macaroni

2 tablespoons unsalted butter

Salt and pepper

¼ teaspoon mustard powder

8 ounces, pasteurized cheese, such as Velveeta®, cut into eighths

2 cups shredded cheddar cheese

Directions:

1. Add 2 cups milk, water, macaroni, butter, and mustard powder to inner pot. Season with salt and pepper. Stir to combine, ensuring pasta is below the water level.

2. Close and lock lid. Adjust pressure valve on top to AIRTIGHT, set COOKING TIME to 7 minutes, and press START.

3. When cooking cycle has finished, release pressure by carefully setting valve to EXHAUST on top of lid. Once all of pressure has released, turn lid, unlock, and open.

4. Add remaining milk and cheeses. Stir to combine. Re-cover and let rest for 5 minutes before serving.

TIP For quick and easy variations, add cooked lobster, crabmeat, diced ham, canned tuna, frozen thawed peas, crumbled hamburger, green onions, or bacon in Step 4 after adding the milk and cheese.

Serves:
8

Prep Time:
15 minutes

**Pressure
Cooking Time:**
6 minutes
(includes
pressure
release time)

Release Method:
NATURAL
& QUICK

Pantry Fried Rice

Why order takeout when this fresh fried rice can be on the table in less time? Better still, it uses basic ingredients you probably already have in your fridge or pantry. Making rice is unbelievably quick in the pressure cooker. After the rice is cooked, quickly scramble a couple of eggs and you're done. It's that easy!

Ingredients:

2 tablespoons sesame oil

1 medium onion, chopped

1 carrot, peeled and chopped

2 cups long-grain white rice, uncooked

3 ½ cups vegetable broth, we recommend Great Flavors® Vegetable Stock Concentrate

¼ cup low-sodium soy sauce

2 cloves garlic, minced

1 cup frozen peas, thawed

3 green onions, chopped

2 large eggs, beaten

Directions:

1. Add sesame oil, onion, carrot, rice, broth, soy sauce, and garlic to inner pot and stir to combine. Close and lock lid. Adjust pressure valve on top to AIRTIGHT, set COOKING TIME to 4 minutes, and press START.

2. When cooking cycle has finished, let the pressure drop NATURALLY for 5 minutes. Release pressure by carefully setting valve to EXHAUST on top of lid. Once all of pressure has released, turn lid and unlock, and open.

3. Add peas and green onions and stir to combine.

4. Set COOKING TIME to 5 minutes and press START. When cooker has heated enough to hear sizzling, push rice against wall of pot creating a hole.

5. Pour beaten eggs into hole and cook, stirring constantly, until set, about 30 seconds. After cooked, stir all ingredients to combine and serve.

TIP For fried rice, it's best to use medium or long-grain rice, which is sturdy and doesn't clump or fall apart after cooking.

Mediterranean Basmati Rice

Serves:
8

Prep Time:
15 minutes

Pressure Cooking Time:
6 minutes

Release Method:
QUICK

This is one of my favorite side dishes to serve with a roast chicken or fish dinner. The combination of tangy apricots and crunchy pistachios makes this dish a standout for any special dinner.

Ingredients:

1 tablespoon vegetable oil

1 medium onion, chopped

2 cups basmati rice, rinsed and drained

3 ½ cups vegetable broth, we recommend Great Flavors® Vegetable Stock Concentrate

½ cup dried apricots, chopped

½ cup pistachios

2 cloves garlic, minced

1 teaspoon ground cumin

½ teaspoon dried sage

Salt and pepper

⅓ cup chopped fresh parsley

Directions:

1. Add oil to inner pot. Set COOKING TIME to 10 minutes and press START. Heat oil about 5 minutes. Add onion and cook until softened, about 5 minutes. Press CANCEL.

2. Add rice, broth, apricots, pistachios, garlic, cumin and sage. Season with salt and pepper and stir to combine. Close and lock lid. Adjust pressure valve on top to AIRTIGHT, set COOKING TIME to 6 minutes, and press START.

3. When cooking cycle has finished, release pressure by carefully setting valve to EXHAUST on top of lid. Once all of pressure has released, turn lid, unlock, and open.

4. Add parsley, and stir to combine.

TIP Rinsing the rice under cold water removes any loose starch left over from the milling process and creates fluffier rice.

Mushroom Risotto

Serves:
8

Prep Time:
15 minutes

Pressure
Cooking Time:
7 minutes

Release Method:
QUICK

A half hour standing over the pot to make risotto? Not anymore! This creamy risotto is so simple to make and is perfect for the mushroom lover. We use fresh mushrooms and mushroom broth to really amp up the mushroom flavor. Serve as a side dish or appetizer with a beef roast or lamb dinner. You only have to stir when it's done to achieve your desired creaminess.

Ingredients:

2 tablespoons unsalted butter

1 medium onion, diced

2 cups Arborio rice

5 cups vegetable broth, we recommend Great Flavors® Vegetable Stock Concentrate

1 pound medium mushrooms, stemmed and sliced

2 cloves garlic, minced

2 bay leaves

⅓ cup grated Parmesan cheese

¼ cup chopped fresh chives

Salt and pepper

Directions:

1. Add butter to inner pot. Set COOKING TIME to 10 minutes and press START. Heat butter until melted, about 5 minutes. Add onion and cook until softened, about 5 minutes. Press CANCEL.

2. Add rice, broth, mushrooms, garlic, and bay leaves and stir to combine. Close and lock lid. Adjust pressure valve on top to AIRTIGHT, set COOKING TIME to 7 minutes, and press START.

3. When cooking cycle has finished, release pressure by carefully setting valve to EXHAUST on top of lid. Once all of pressure has released, turn lid, unlock, and open.

4. Stir in Parmesan cheese and chives. Season with salt and pepper. To make the risotto creamier, simply stir vigorously until desired creaminess is achieved.

TIP Any leftover risotto can be turned into another meal. Refrigerate until cold and firm. Form small burger-shaped patties, adding shredded cheese, if you'd like. Pan fry in butter until crispy on both sides then bake in a 350°F oven until hot.

Serves:
12

Prep Time:
15 minutes

Pressure Cooking Time:
6 minutes

Release Method:
QUICK

 # Brown Rice Pilaf

Brown rice is a tasty whole grain, rich in fiber and anti-oxidants, with a unique nutty flavor. The pressure cooker does its magic in preparing brown rice in no time. The addition of herbs, spices, and flavorful vegetable broth makes this extra delicious.

Ingredients:

1 tablespoon vegetable oil

1 medium onion, chopped

3 ½ cups vegetable broth, we recommend Great Flavors® Vegetable Stock Concentrate

2 cups brown rice

2 cloves garlic, minced

2 tablespoons minced fresh thyme

Salt and pepper

⅓ cup chopped fresh parsley

Directions:

1. Add oil to inner pot. Set COOKING TIME to 15 minutes and press START. Heat oil about 5 minutes. Add onion and cook until softened, about 10 minutes. Press CANCEL.

2. Add broth, rice, garlic, and thyme. Season with salt and pepper, and stir to combine. Close and lock lid. Adjust pressure valve on top to AIRTIGHT, set COOKING TIME to 6 minutes, and press START.

3. When cooking cycle had finished, release pressure by carefully setting valve to EXHAUST on top of lid. Once all of pressure has released, turn lid, unlock, and open.

4. Add parsley and season with salt and pepper.

Confetti Quinoa

Serves:
10 to 12

Prep Time:
20 minutes

Pressure Cooking Time:
6 minutes

Release Method:
QUICK

Quinoa is one of my favorite grains, full of protein and flavor. Adding a rainbow of vegetables creates one beautiful, healthy, and delicious side dish. Add cooked chicken or shrimp to make a complete meal.

Ingredients:

2 cups quinoa

3 cups vegetable broth, we recommend Great Flavors® Vegetable Stock Concentrate

1 red bell pepper, seeded and diced

1 yellow bell pepper, seeded and diced

2 cups chopped broccoli

1 cup frozen corn, thawed

3 tablespoons extra-virgin olive oil

Salt and pepper

2 tomatoes, seeded and chopped

¼ cup chopped green onion

Directions:

1. Add quinoa, broth, red and yellow pepper, broccoli, corn and olive oil to inner pot. Season with salt and pepper, and stir to combine. Close and lock lid. Adjust pressure valve on top to AIRTIGHT, set COOKING TIME to 6 minutes, and press START.

2. When cooking cycle has finished, release pressure by carefully setting valve to EXHAUST on top of lid. Once all of pressure has released, turn lid, unlock, and open.

3. Add tomatoes and green onions. Stir to combine.

TIP Top with crumbled Feta cheese, grated Parmesan, or any fresh Mexican crumbly cheese.

Brown Rice Breakfast Bowl

Serves:
8

Prep Time:
5 minutes

Pressure Cooking Time:
10 minutes

Release Method:
QUICK

Hearty brown rice makes a perfect breakfast, giving you satisfying whole grains filled with fiber. Select your favorite mix-ins! Choose your mix-ins by the fruit of the season, and add a little sugar and spice.

Ingredients:

2 cups brown rice

2 ½ cups water

1 ½ cups milk

⅛ teaspoon salt

MIX-INS

¼ cup dark brown sugar

¼ cup maple syrup

¼ cup honey

2 teaspoons vanilla extract

1½ teaspoons cinnamon

TOPPINGS

2 cups blueberries, raspberries, sliced strawberries, or diced apples

2 ripe bananas, chopped

½ cup raisins, chopped almonds, or chopped walnuts

Directions:

1. Add all ingredients including any mix-ins, if using, to inner pot and stir to combine. Close and lock the lid. Adjust pressure valve on top to AIRTIGHT, set COOKING TIME to 10 minutes, and press START.

2. When cooking cycle has finished, release pressure by carefully setting valve to EXHAUST on top of lid. Once all of pressure has released, turn lid, unlock, and open. Add toppings, if desired

Serves:
8 to 10

Prep Time:
10 minutes

Pressure Cooking Time:
9 minutes

Release Method:
QUICK

Creamy Polenta

Creamy polenta is a comforting Italian side dish that makes a great bed for slow-cooked meaty ragu or rich short ribs. The finishing touch of herbed cream cheese adds extra creaminess.

Ingredients:

1 tablespoon vegetable oil

1 medium onion, minced

5 ½ cups chicken broth, we recommend Great Flavors® Chicken Stock Concentrate

1 ¾ cups stone-ground yellow cornmeal

¼ teaspoon garlic powder

Salt and pepper

4 ounces herb & garlic cream cheese, softened

Directions:

1. Add oil to inner pot. Set COOKING TIME to 10 minutes and press START. Heat oil about 5 minutes. Add onion and cook until softened, about 5 minutes. Press CANCEL.

2. Add broth, cornmeal, and garlic powder and stir to combine. Close and lock lid. Adjust pressure valve on top to AIRTIGHT, set COOKING TIME to 9 minutes, and press START.

3. When cooking cycle has finished, release pressure by carefully setting valve to EXHAUST on top of lid. Once all of pressure has released, turn lid, unlock, and open.

4. Whisk in cream cheese and serve.

TIP Be imaginative when deciding what to add to the polenta. Consider peas, zucchini, mushrooms, truffle oil, cooked shredded short ribs, or even shrimp.

Chana Masala

Serves:
8 to 10

Prep Time:
15 minutes

**Pressure
Cooking Time:**
50 minutes
(Includes
pressure
release time)

Release Method:
NATURAL

The pressure cooker will be your new best friend when cooking dried beans, as they cook in no time and don't require pre-soaking. This savory Indian dish may introduce you to a new and flavorful ingredient, Garam Masala, which can be found in the spice aisle in your supermarket.

Ingredients:

3 cups dried chickpeas

1 tablespoon vegetable oil

1 medium onion, chopped

3 cups vegetable broth, we recommend Great Flavors® Vegetable Stock Concentrate

1¼ teaspoons Garam Masala

1 teaspoon minced fresh ginger

1 teaspoon cumin

1 teaspoon ground coriander

2 large tomatoes, seeded and chopped

¼ cup minced fresh cilantro

Salt and pepper

Directions:

1. Add chickpeas to inner pot and cover with water by 1 inch. Close and lock lid. Adjust pressure valve on top to AIRTIGHT, set COOKING TIME to 4 minutes, and press START.

2. When cooking cycle has finished, let pressure drop NATURALLY. Drain chickpeas and set aside.

3. Add oil to inner pot. Set COOKING TIME to 15 minutes and press START. Heat oil for 5 minutes, then add onion to inner pot, and cook until softened, about 10 minutes. Press CANCEL.

4. Add chickpeas, broth, Garam Masala, ginger, cumin, and coriander and stir to combine. Close and lock lid. Adjust pressure valve on top to AIRTIGHT, set COOKING TIME to 25 minutes, and press START.

5. When cooking cycle has finished, release pressure by carefully setting valve to EXHAUST on top of lid. Once all of pressure has released, turn lid, unlock, and open.

6. Add tomatoes and cilantro and season with salt and pepper. Stir to combine.

TIP In India, this dish is eaten for breakfast, a main meal, or as a snack. Try adding different spices such as turmeric, chili powder, cloves, or cardamom. Each will give a unique flavor to this vegetarian dish.

Barbecue Baked Beans

Serves:
10 to 12

Prep Time:
15 minutes

Pressure Cooking Time:
45 minutes

Release Method:
QUICK

This BBQ favorite is so simple and FAST to make in the pressure cooker. It's amazing how dried beans can be cooked in just minutes! The addition of bacon, peppers, and onions add intense and homemade flavor to the barbecue sauce.

Ingredients:

1 pound small navy beans, rinsed and picked over

1 tablespoon vegetable oil

½ pound bacon, diced

1 medium onion, diced

1 green bell pepper, seeded and chopped

3 cups chicken broth, we recommend Great Flavors® Chicken Concentrate

1 (18 oz.) bottle barbecue sauce, divided

Directions:

1. Add beans to inner pot and cover with water by 1 inch. Close and lock lid. Adjust pressure valve on top to AIRTIGHT, set COOKING TIME to 4 minutes, and press START. When cooking cycle has finished, let pressure drop NATURALLY. Drain beans and set aside.

2. Add oil to inner pot. Set COOKING TIME to 15 minutes and press START. Heat oil about 5 minutes. Add bacon and cook until browned, about 10 minutes. Press CANCEL.

3. Add reserved beans, onion, green pepper, broth and half of barbecue sauce. Stir to combine. Close and lock lid. Adjust pressure valve on top to AIRTIGHT, set COOKING TIME to 20 minutes, and press START.

4. When cooking cycle has finished, release pressure by carefully setting valve to EXHAUST on top of lid. Once all of pressure has released, turn lid, unlock, and open.

5. Add remaining barbecue sauce and stir to combine.

TIP Instead of cooking the beans in Step 1, you can soak them overnight and add them in Step 3. In a large bowl, cover beans with at least 3 inches of water. Refrigerate and soak overnight. Drain and rinse.

Serves:
10 to 12

Prep Time:
10 minutes

**Pressure
Cooking Time:**
45 minutes
(Includes
pressure
release time)

Release Method:
NATURAL
& QUICK

Black Eyed Peas

These Southern gems, typically served on New Year's Day for good luck, are seasoned with smoky paprika and ham to complement the earthy nuttiness of the beans. No need to pre-soak them for hours! Using the pressure cooker, the dish is done in a little over a half hour.

Ingredients:

1 pound dried black-eyed peas, rinsed and picked over

1 tablespoon vegetable oil

1 medium onion, diced

6 ounces smoked ham steak, diced

2 cups chicken broth, we recommend Great Flavors® Chicken Stock Concentrate

2 cloves garlic, minced

2 bay leaves

1 teaspoon smoked paprika

Salt and pepper

Directions:

1. Add black-eyed peas to inner pot and cover with water by 1 inch. Close and lock lid. Adjust pressure valve on top to AIRTIGHT, set COOKING TIME to 4 minutes, and press START. When cooking cycle has finished, let pressure drop NATURALLY. Drain peas and set aside.

2. Add oil to inner pot. Set COOKING TIME to 10 minutes and press START. Heat oil about 5 minutes. Add onion and cook until softened, about 5 minutes. Press CANCEL.

3. Add black-eyed peas, ham, broth, garlic, bay leaves, and paprika and stir to combine. Close and lock lid, adjust the pressure valve on top to AIRTIGHT, set COOKING TIME to 20 minutes, and press START.

4. When cooking cycle has finished, release pressure by carefully setting valve to EXHAUST on top of lid. Once all of pressure has released, turn lid, unlock, and open. Season with salt and pepper.

SIDES

Potatoes Au Gratin, 151

Serves:
6 to 8

Prep Time:
10 minutes

**Pressure
Cooking Time:**
4 minutes

Release Method:
QUICK

Balsamic Glazed Carrots

Sweet brown sugar and tangy orange juice create a flavorful glaze for the carrots. Adding a final drizzle of rich balsamic glaze makes them totally addictive.

Ingredients:

3 tablespoons unsalted butter

1 medium onion, minced

1 clove garlic, minced

8 large carrots, peeled, cut into ½-inch rounds

⅔ cup water

⅔ cup orange juice

2 tablespoons light brown sugar

Salt and pepper

Balsamic glaze for garnish

Fresh thyme leaves for garnish

Directions:

1. Add butter to inner pot. Set COOKING TIME to 10 minutes and press START. Heat butter until melted, about 5 minutes. Add onion and garlic and cook until softened, about 4 minutes. Press CANCEL.

2. Add carrots, water, orange juice, and brown sugar. Season with salt and pepper. Close and lock lid. Adjust the pressure valve on top to AIRTIGHT, set COOKING TIME to 4 minutes, and press START.

3. When cooking cycle has finished, release pressure by carefully setting valve to EXHAUST on top of lid. Once all of pressure has released, turn lid, unlock, and open.

4. Drain cooking liquid. Season with salt and pepper. Transfer carrots to serving dish and garnish with balsamic glaze and thyme.

TIP **Balsamic glaze can be found in the Italian aisle of the supermarket.**

Glazed Root Vegetables

Serves:
10

Prep Time:
10 minutes

Pressure Cooking Time:
4 minutes

Release Method:
QUICK

Your holiday table should definitely include these sweet and savory vegetables. And they cook in only 4 minutes. Try the fall variety shown below or experiment with other combinations throughout the winter months.

Ingredients:

4 tablespoons unsalted butter

1 medium onion, chopped

2 pounds parsnips, peeled, and cut into 1-inch chunks

1 pound baby carrots

⅓ cup honey

¼ cup water

1 tablespoon minced fresh rosemary

Salt and pepper

Directions:

1. Add all ingredients, in the order listed, to inner pot. Close and lock lid. Adjust pressure valve on top to AIRTIGHT, set COOKING TIME to 4 minutes, and press START.

2. When cooking cycle has finished, release pressure by carefully setting valve to EXHAUST on top of lid. Once all of pressure has released, turn lid, unlock, and open. Season with salt and pepper.

TIP For flavors of autumn, omit the honey and rosemary. Instead, add ¼ cup maple syrup, ¼ teaspoon cinnamon, and ⅛ teaspoon nutmeg.

Stewed Ratatouille

All of the vegetables and seasonings meld together under pressure to provide the ultimate flavorful and healthy dish. Plus, it only takes 4 minutes to cook! Serve as a side or with brown rice or quinoa as a meal.

Serves:
8 to 10

Prep Time:
20 minutes

Pressure Cooking Time:
4 minutes

Release Method:
QUICK

Ingredients:

3 tablespoons olive oil

1 medium onion, chopped

2 cloves garlic, minced

1 red bell pepper, seeded, cut into 1-inch chunks

1 yellow bell pepper, seeded, cut into 1-inch chunks

1 large zucchini, cut into 1-inch chunks

1 large eggplant, cut into 1-inch chunks

1 (14 oz.) can crushed tomatoes

1 (14 oz.) can diced tomatoes, drained

1 tablespoon Italian seasoning, we recommend Great Flavors® Italian Seasoning

Salt and pepper

Directions:

1. Add oil to inner pot. Set COOKING TIME to 10 minutes and press START. Heat oil about 5 minutes. Add onion, garlic, and peppers and cook until just softened, about 2 minutes.

2. Add zucchini, eggplant, Italian seasoning, and both canned tomatoes. Stir to combine ingredients. Season with salt and pepper. Press CANCEL.

3. Close and lock lid. Adjust pressure valve on top to AIRTIGHT, set COOKING TIME to 4 minutes, and press START.

4. When cooking cycle has finished, release pressure by carefully setting valve to EXHAUST on top of lid. Once all of pressure has released, turn lid, unlock, and open.

TIP Though classic ratatouille is simmered over a long period of time the pressure cooker develops the same rich sauce and depth of flavor in a lot less time.

Serves:
8

Prep Time:
15 minutes

Pressure
Cooking Time:
15 minutes

Release Method:
QUICK

 N'Orleans Greens

You know it's important to eat your greens, right? The bitterness of the collards is mellowed by sugar and heat—and lots of it! This spicy side will have you begging for more greens.

Ingredients:

3 tablespoons olive oil

1 medium onion, minced

4 cloves garlic, minced

3 bunches collard greens, rinsed well, stemmed, and coarsely chopped

1 (14.5 oz.) can diced tomatoes, drained

½ cup vegetable broth, we recommend Great Flavors® Vegetable Stock Concentrate

¼ cup apple cider vinegar

2 tablespoons Louisiana hot sauce

1 tablespoon light brown sugar

Salt and pepper

Directions:

1. Add oil to inner pot. Set COOKING TIME to 15 minutes and press START. Heat oil about 5 minutes. Add onion, garlic, and ½ the collard greens and cook until wilted, about 5 minutes. Add remaining ½ collard greens and continue cooking until softened, about 5 more minutes. Press CANCEL.

2. Add tomatoes, broth, vinegar, hot sauce, and brown sugar and stir to combine.

3. Close and lock lid. Adjust pressure valve on top to AIRTIGHT, set COOKING TIME to 15 minutes, and press START.

4. When cooking cycle has finished, release pressure by carefully setting valve to EXHAUST on top of lid. Once all of pressure has released, turn lid, unlock, and open. Season with salt and pepper.

TIP If you can't find collard greens, kale or Swiss chard can be substituted here.

Balsamic & Bacon Green Beans

These will be the best green beans you will ever eat! The combination of savory onions and garlic and smoky bacon are taken to another level with a final drizzle of balsamic glaze.

Serves:
8 to 10

Prep Time:
15 minutes

Pressure Cooking Time:
3 minutes

Release Method:
QUICK

Ingredients:

1 tablespoon vegetable oil

8 slices thick-cut bacon, cut into ½-inch pieces

1 medium onion, thinly sliced

2 cloves garlic, minced

2 pounds green beans, trimmed

½ cup vegetable broth, we recommend Great Flavors® Vegetable Stock Concentrate

Salt and pepper

2 tablespoons balsamic glaze

Directions:

1. Add oil to inner pot. Set COOKING TIME to 15 minutes and press START. Heat oil about 5 minutes. Add bacon and cook until browned, about 10 minutes. Press CANCEL.

2. Add onion, garlic, green beans, and broth. Season with salt and pepper. Close and lock lid. Adjust pressure valve on top to AIRTIGHT, set COOKING TIME to 3 minutes, and press START.

3. When cooking cycle has finished, release pressure by carefully setting valve to EXHAUST on top of lid. Once all of pressure has released, turn lid, unlock, and open.

4. Transfer green beans to serving dish. Drizzle with balsamic glaze.

TIP **For a vegetarian version, omit the bacon.**

# Pickled Beets

Makes:
1 ¼ quarts

Prep Time:
20 minutes

Pressure Cooking Time:
10 minutes

Release Method:
QUICK

Beets are a traditional Midwestern favorite. The aromatic spice mix added to the vinegar enhances the natural sweetness of the beets. The vinegar also helps the beets last longer in the fridge.

Ingredients:

8 large beets, scrubbed, and cut into 2-inch pieces

1 large red onion, chopped

1 cup apple cider vinegar

¼ cup water

⅔ cup sugar

2 bay leaves

½ teaspoon ground cinnamon

¼ teaspoon ground cloves

¼ teaspoon dry mustard

⅛ teaspoon ground allspice

2 teaspoons salt

Directions:

1. Add all ingredients, in the order listed, to inner pot and stir until combined. Close and lock lid. Adjust pressure valve on top to AIRTIGHT, set COOKING TIME to 10 minutes, and press START.

2. When cooking cycle has finished, release pressure by carefully setting valve to EXHAUST on top of lid. Once all of pressure has released, turn lid, unlock, and open.

3. Transfer mixture to airtight container and refrigerate until cold, about 2 hours. Cool completely before serving.

TIP When selecting beets make sure they are firm and unblemished. If the leaves are attached, make sure they are not wilted.

Serves:
8

Prep Time:
10 minutes

Pressure Cooking Time:
7 minutes

Release Method:
QUICK

 # Mediterranean-Style Cauliflower

Want a change from a traditional dinner salad? The pressure cooker can cook a whole head of cauliflower in only 7 minutes. Drizzle our tangy, lemon garlic dressing over the top and section off pieces for a delicious side.

Ingredients:

1 head cauliflower, core removed

⅓ cup extra-virgin olive oil

¼ cup sliced toasted almonds

¼ cup chopped green onion

3 tablespoon fresh lemon juice

2 cloves garlic, minced

2 tablespoons minced fresh rosemary

Salt and pepper

Directions:

1. Place cauliflower on wire rack. Add 1 ½ cups water to inner pot. Close and lock lid. Adjust pressure valve on top to AIRTIGHT, set COOKING TIME to 7 minutes, and press START.

2. When cooking cycle has finished, release pressure by carefully setting valve to EXHAUST on top of lid. Once all of pressure has released, turn lid, unlock, and open.

3. In a small bowl, combine oil, almonds, green onion, lemon, garlic, and rosemary. Season with salt and pepper.

4. Transfer cauliflower to serving dish and season with salt and pepper. Top with almond mixture.

TIP This is a great dish to serve at a dinner party. Serve whole, and cut the cauliflower into wedges with the savory sauce.

Potatoes Au Gratin

This potato dish is the ultimate in comfort food—gooey, rich, and cheesy. The addition of the crushed cracker topping adds extra flavor and texture to this classic.

Serves:
10 to 12

Prep Time:
20 minutes

Pressure Cooking Time:
9 minutes

Release Method:
QUICK

Ingredients:

3 tablespoons unsalted butter

1 medium onion, finely chopped

3 cloves garlic, minced

1 cup chicken broth, we recommend Great Flavors® Chicken Stock Concentrate

1 cup light cream

1 tablespoon minced fresh rosemary

2 ½ pounds russet potatoes, thinly sliced, divided

Salt and pepper

1 ½ cups shredded Parmesan cheese, divided

1 cup crushed buttery crackers

Directions:

1. Add butter to inner pot. Set COOKING TIME to 10 minutes and press START. Heat butter until melted, about 5 minutes. Add onion and garlic and cook until softened, about 5 minutes. Press CANCEL.

2. In a medium bowl, combine broth, cream, and rosemary.

3. Layer ⅓ of the potato slices in inner pot, and season with salt and pepper. Add ⅓ of the cream mixture, coating potatoes evenly with the liquid. Sprinkle with ½ cup Parmesan cheese. Repeat with 2 more layers.

4. Close and lock lid. Adjust pressure valve on top to AIRTIGHT, set COOKING TIME to 9 minutes, and press START.

5. When cooking cycle has finished, release pressure by carefully setting valve to EXHAUST on top of lid. Once all of pressure has released, turn lid, unlock, and open.

6. Transfer potatoes to serving dish. Sprinkle with buttery crackers.

TIP To get a crispy cheese crust, transfer potatoes to an oven safe casserole dish and top with 1½ cups shredded cheddar cheese. Place under broiler until cheese is melted and browned.

Sweet Potato Streusel

Serves:
8

Prep Time:
20 minutes

Pressure
Cooking Time:
17 minutes

Release Method:
QUICK

Thanksgiving would never be the same without a rich and gooey sweet potato side dish. The pressure cooker does a great job cooking the sweet potatoes in less than 20 minutes and the streusel topping combines sweet, spicy, and salty perfectly.

Ingredients:

4 tablespoons unsalted butter, softened

¾ cup all-purpose flour

¼ cup sugar

2 tablespoons light brown sugar

¼ teaspoon cinnamon

⅛ teaspoon salt

½ cup walnut pieces

8 small sweet potatoes, scrubbed

1 cup mini marshmallows

⅓ cup maple syrup

Directions:

1. Preheat oven to 350°F. Line a cookie sheet with parchment paper.

2. In a medium bowl, combine butter, flour, both sugars, cinnamon, salt, and walnuts until mixture resembles coarse crumbs. Transfer mixture to cookie sheet and bake until light golden brown, about 15 minutes. Let cool completely.

3. Place sweet potatoes on wire rack in pressure cooker. Add 1 ½ cups water to inner pot. Close and lock lid. Adjust pressure valve on top to AIRTIGHT, set COOKING TIME to 17 minutes, and press START.

4. When cooking cycle has finished, release pressure by carefully setting valve to EXHAUST on top of lid. Once all of pressure has released, turn lid, unlock, and open.

5. Transfer sweet potatoes to serving dish. Cut slit in center of each sweet potato. Top with marshmallows and streusel. Drizzle with maple syrup.

TIP **For nut-free diets, walnuts can easily be eliminated.**

Serves:
8 to 10

Prep Time:
15 minutes

Pressure Cooking Time:
6 minutes

Release Method:
QUICK

Classic Mashed Potatoes

This is the best way to make mashed potatoes... in 6 minutes! Sour cream and potatoes go hand-in-hand so we added a bit here to balance the richness of the butter and milk. Creamy and delicious!

Ingredients:

5 pounds medium red potatoes, cut into 2-inch pieces

2 cups water

8 tablespooons (1 stick) unsalted butter, softened

1 ¾ cups warm milk

⅔ cup sour cream

Salt and pepper

Directions:

1. Add potatoes and water to inner pot. Close and lock lid. Adjust pressure valve on top to AIRTIGHT, set COOKING TIME to 6 minutes, and press START.

2. When cooking cycle has finished, release pressure by carefully setting valve to EXHAUST on top of lid. Once all of pressure has released, turn lid, unlock, and open.

3. Drain cooked potatoes and return to pot. Add butter, milk, and sour cream.

4. Using a potato masher, mash potatoes until smooth. Season with salt and pepper.

TIP For added texture and flavor, top with cooked bacon or scallions or add 6 ounces goat cheese with butter in Step 3.

DESSERTS

Baked Apples, 173

Flourless Chocolate Cake

Serves:
8

Prep Time:
20 minutes

Pressure Cooking Time:
45 minutes (includes pressure release time)

Release Method:
NATURAL

No chocolate lover's GLUTEN FREE dessert ever tasted so good. This dessert is ultra-rich from the combination of the chocolate and butter and has intense chocolate flavor. Cut into small squares to get your daily chocolate fix!

Ingredients:

10 ounces semi-sweet chocolate, chopped

8 tablespoons (1 stick) unsalted butter

4 large eggs

1/2 cup sugar

1 teaspoon vanilla extract

1/8 teaspoon salt

Directions:

1. Spray an 8-inch springform pan with nonstick cooking spray. Line bottom of pan with parchment paper and spray again. Set aside.

2. Over low heat, melt chocolate and butter in small saucepan. Remove from heat.

3. In a large bowl, using an electric mixer, beat eggs, sugar, vanilla, and salt until pale yellow and thick, 6 to 8 minutes.

4. Fold melted chocolate mixture into egg mixture until just incorporated. Pour batter into prepared pan.

5. Tightly cover top of pan completely with lightly greased aluminum foil. Place small rack in inner pot. Add 2 cups of water. Place cake pan on rack.

6. Close and lock lid. Adjust pressure valve on top to AIRTIGHT, set COOKING TIME to 25 minutes, and press START.

7. When cooking cycle has finished, let pressure drop NATURALLY and let cake sit inside turned off pressure cooker for 20 minutes. Turn lid, unlock, and open.

8. Remove cake from inner pot and remove foil. Let cool completely. Refrigerate for 3 hours before serving.

TIP Serve with fresh berries and a sprinkle of confectioners sugar.

Peach Cake

You will have another reason to look forward to summer, knowing that you can make this delicious cake. The natural sweetness and texture of the peaches are both inside the cake and on top.

Serves:
8 to 10

Prep Time:
25 minutes

Pressure Cooking Time:
1 hour
(includes pressure release time)

Release Method:
NATURAL

Ingredients:

2 cups fresh peach slices

2 tablespoons dark brown sugar

1 ½ cups all-purpose flour

½ teaspoon baking powder

½ teaspoon baking soda

¼ teaspoon salt

2 large eggs

1 cup sugar

½ cup peach nectar

1 teaspoon almond extract

¼ cup vegetable oil

Directions:

1. Spray an 8-inch x 3-inch round cake pan with nonstick cooking spray.

2. Toss peach slices with brown sugar and place half of slices at bottom of pan.

3. In a small bowl, whisk flour, baking powder, baking soda, and salt. Set aside.

4. In a large bowl, using an electric mixer, beat the eggs, sugar, peach nectar, almond extract, and oil until well combined.

5. Add the dry ingredients to wet ingredients and beat until just incorporated. Fold remaining peach slices into cake batter. Pour cake batter into prepared pan.

6. Tightly cover top of pan completely with lightly greased aluminum foil. Place small rack in inner pot. Add 2 cups of water. Place cake pan on rack.

7. Close and lock lid. Adjust pressure valve on top to AIRTIGHT, set COOKING TIME to 35 minutes, and press START.

8. When cooking cycle has finished, let pressure drop NATURALLY. Once all of pressure has released, turn lid, unlock, and open. Remove cake from pot and remove foil.

9. Let cool for 10 minutes before unmolding onto a cake platter. Cool completely before serving.

TIP For a wonderful glaze on the cake, whisk 1 ¼ cups confectioners sugar, 3 tablespoons milk, and ½ teaspoon vanilla extract until smooth and pour over cake.

Pineapple Upside Down Cake

This cake comes out so beautifully and showcases the delicious brown sugar-coated pineapple rings. The moist cake texture makes this dessert a true winner. .

Serves:
8

Prep Time:
25 minutes

Pressure Cooking Time:
50 minutes (includes pressure release time)

Release Method:
NATURAL

Ingredients:

5 slices canned pineapple, reserving ½ cup liquid

3 tablespoons dark brown sugar

1 ⅓ cups all-purpose flour

½ teaspoon baking powder

½ teaspoon baking soda

¼ teaspoon salt

3 large eggs

1 cup sugar

1 tablespoon vanilla extract

¼ cup vegetable oil

¼ cup caramel sauce for garnish

Directions:

1. Spray an 8-inch x 3-inch round cake pan with nonstick cooking spray.

2. In a small bowl, toss pineapple slices with brown sugar. Place slices at bottom of pan and top with any remaining sugar in bowl.

3. In another small bowl, whisk flour, baking powder, baking soda, and salt. Set aside.

4. In a large bowl, using an electric mixer, beat eggs, sugar, reserved pineapple juice, vanilla, and oil until well combined.

5. Add dry ingredients to wet ingredients and beat until just incorporated. Pour cake batter into prepared pan.

6. Tightly cover top of pan completely with lightly greased aluminum foil. Place small rack in inner pot. Add 2 cups of water. Place cake pan on rack.

7. Close and lock lid. Adjust pressure valve on top to AIRTIGHT, set COOKING TIME to 30 minutes, and press START.

8. When pressure cooker has finished cooking cycle, let pressure drop NATURALLY. Once all of pressure has released, turn lid, unlock, and open.

9. Remove cake from inner pot and remove foil. Let cool 10 minutes before unmolding onto cake platter. Cool completely. Drizzle with caramel sauce before serving.

> **TIP** Try making pear upside down cake instead. Substitute canned pears for the pineapple, reserve pear juice, and add dried cranberries and a ¼ teaspoon pumpkin pie spice.

Marble-ous Cheesecake

Be creative making this cheesecake making unique chocolate swirls throughout the cheesecake batter. You will definitely enjoy this slice of heaven...simply marble-ous!

Serves:
8 to 10

Prep Time:
15 minutes

Pressure Cooking Time:
1 hour,
10 minutes

Release Method:
NATURAL

Ingredients:

9 chocolate graham crackers, crushed

4 tablespoons unsalted butter, melted

1 pound cream cheese, softened

¾ cup sugar

1 teaspoon vanilla extract

3 large eggs

4 ounces semi-sweet chocolate chips, melted

Directions:

1. Spray an 8-inch springform pan with nonstick cooking spray. Line bottom with piece of parchment paper and spray again. Set aside.

2. In a small bowl, mix the crushed graham crackers and melted butter. Press mixture into bottom of prepared pan. Set aside.

3. In a large bowl, using an electric mixer, beat the cream cheese until light and fluffy. Add sugar and vanilla and beat until smooth and no lumps remain.

4. Add eggs, one at a time, until evenly incorporated. Remove ⅓ of cheesecake batter and place in a small bowl. Add melted chocolate chips and stir to combine.

5. Pour plain cheesecake batter into prepared pan, dollop the chocolate cheesecake mixture on top. Using a small, thin spatula, gently swirl the batters to create a marble effect.

6. Tightly cover top of pan completely with lightly greased aluminum foil. Place small rack in pot. Add 2 cups of water. Place cake pan on rack.

7. Close and lock lid. Adjust pressure valve on top to AIRTIGHT, set COOKING TIME to 25 minutes, and press START.

8. When cooking cycle has finished, let pressure drop NATURALLY. Let cheesecake sit inside turned off pressure cooker for 45 minutes. Turn lid, unlock, and open.

9. Remove cheesecake from pot and remove foil. Wrap cheesecake with plastic wrap. Refrigerate for 8 hours or overnight. Let cheesecake sit at room temperature for at least 1 hour before cutting and serving.

TIP You can substitute milk chocolate chips for a sweeter taste or dark chocolate chips for more intense chocolate flavor.

Serves:
8 to 10

Prep Time:
15 minutes

Pressure
Cooking Time:
1 hour,
15 minutes

Release Method:
NATURAL

Cappuccino Cheesecake

Cheesecake in a pressure cooker? Yes! The combination of cream cheese and whipping cream provides the ultimate in creaminess, and the espresso granules and vanilla adds the cappuccino richness.

Ingredients:

9 graham crackers, crushed

4 tablespoons unsalted butter, melted

1/4 cup whipping cream

1 tablespoon instant espresso granules

1 teaspoon vanilla extract

1 pound cream cheese, softened

3/4 cup sugar

3 large eggs

Whipped cream for garnish

1 tablespoon finely ground coffee beans for garnish

Directions:

1. Spray an 8-inch springform pan with nonstick cooking spray. Line bottom with piece of parchment paper and spray again. Set aside.

2. In a small bowl, mix crushed graham crackers and melted butter. Press mixture into bottom of prepared pan. Set aside.

3. In a separate small bowl, combine cream, espresso powder, and vanilla. Set aside.

4. In a large bowl, using an electric mixer, beat the cream cheese until light and fluffy. Add sugar and beat until smooth and no lumps remain. Add espresso mixture until powder dissolves into cream cheese mixture.

5. Add eggs, one at a time, until evenly incorporated. Pour cheesecake batter into prepared pan.

6. Tightly cover top of pan completely with lightly greased aluminum foil. Place small rack in inner pot. Add 2 cups of water. Place cake pan on rack.

7. Close and lock lid. Adjust pressure valve on top to AIRTIGHT, set COOKING TIME to 30 minutes, and press START.

8. When cooking cycle has finished, let pressure drop NATURALLY. Let cheesecake sit inside turned off pressure cooker for 45 minutes. Turn lid, unlock, and open.

9. Remove cheesecake from pot and remove foil. Wrap cheesecake with plastic wrap. Refrigerate for 8 hours or overnight.

10. Let cheesecake sit at room temperature for at least 30 minutes before cutting. Pipe or dollop whipped cream on top of cheesecake around border and sprinkle with ground coffee.

Triple Chocolate Peanut Butter Cheesecake

Serves: 10 to 12

Prep Time: 15 minutes

Pressure Cooking Time: 1 hour, 20 minutes

Release Method: NATURAL

This cheesecake is one of the most decadent desserts you will ever make—perfect for any celebration. The triple chocolate hit in the crust, batter, and candy additions plus the double dose of peanut butter makes this dessert ultra rich...and ultra good.

Ingredients:

1 ½ cups crushed Oreo® cookies

2 tablespoons unsalted butter, melted

1 pound cream cheese, softened

¾ cup sugar

⅓ cup creamy peanut butter

2 large eggs

12 peanut butter cups, chopped, divided

⅔ cup chocolate sauce

Directions:

1. Spray an 8-inch springform pan with nonstick cooking spray. Line bottom with piece of parchment paper and spray again. Set aside.

2. In a small bowl, mix the crushed Oreos® and melted butter. Press mixture into bottom of prepared pan. Sprinkle half of the chopped peanut butter cups over the crust. Set aside.

3. In a large bowl, using an electric mixer, beat cream cheese until light and fluffy. Add sugar and peanut butter and beat until smooth.

4. Add eggs, one at a time, and beat until evenly incorporated. Pour cheesecake batter into prepared pan.

5. Tightly cover top of pan completely with lightly greased aluminum foil. Place small rack in pot. Add 2 cups of water. Place cake pan on rack.

6. Close and lock lid. Adjust pressure valve on top to AIRTIGHT, set COOKING TIME to 30 minutes, and press START.

7. When cooking cycle has finished, let pressure drop NATURALLY. Let cheesecake sit inside turned off pressure cooker for 50 minutes. Turn lid, unlock, and open.

8. Remove cheesecake from pot and remove foil. Wrap cheesecake with plastic wrap. Refrigerate for 8 hours or overnight.

9. Top cheesecake with remaining chopped peanut butter cups and drizzle with chocolate sauce. Let sit at room temperature for at least 30 minutes before cutting and serving.

TIP **Caramel sauce can be substituted for the chocolate sauce.**

Serves:
6 to 8

Prep Time:
10 minutes

Pressure Cooking Time:
25 minutes (includes pressure release time)

Release Method:
NATURAL

Cherry Cheesecake Rice Pudding

The cream cheese, vanilla, and nutmeg added to this recipe deliver the rich and creamy cheesecake flavor. The cherry pie filling is a fabulous finishing touch, bringing you the classic diner dessert!

Ingredients:

4 ⅔ cups milk, divided

2 cups half-and-half

1 ½ cups short-grain white rice

1 cup sugar

1 tablespoon vanilla extract

⅛ teaspoon salt

Pinch ground nutmeg

1 (8 oz.) package cream cheese, softened

1 (21 oz.) can cherry pie filling

Directions:

1. Add 2 ⅔ cups milk, half-and-half, rice, sugar, vanilla, salt, and nutmeg to inner pot and stir to combine. Close and lock lid. Adjust pressure valve on top to AIRTIGHT, set COOKING TIME to 5 minutes, and press START.

2. When cooking cycle has finished, let pressure drop NATURALLY. Once all of pressure has released, turn lid, unlock, and open.

3. Add cream cheese and remaining milk and stir to combine, ensuring no chunks of cream cheese remain. Transfer rice pudding to airtight container and refrigerate 2 hours or until cold.

4. Top each serving with cherry pie filling.

TIP You can substitute any pie filling for cherry in this recipe.

Rum Raisin Rice Pudding

Serves:
6 to 8

Prep Time:
10 minutes

Pressure Cooking Time:
25 minutes (includes pressure release time)

Release Method:
NATURAL

This comforting dessert has so much flavor thanks to the addition of raisins, which soak up the rum during cooking. Top with a dollop of whipped cream for dessert or serve it for Sunday brunch.

Ingredients:

4 cups milk, divided

2 cups half-and-half

¾ cup sugar

1 ½ cups short-grain white rice

1 tablespoon vanilla extract

1 teaspoon ground cinnamon

1 ¼ cups raisins

½ cup dark rum

Directions:

1. Add 2 cups milk, half-and-half, sugar, rice, vanilla, cinnamon, raisins, and rum to inner pot, and stir to combine. Close and lock lid. Adjust pressure valve on top to AIRTIGHT, set COOKING TIME to 5 minutes, and press START.

2. When cooking cycle has finished, let pressure drop NATURALLY. Once all of pressure has released, turn lid, unlock, and open.

3. Add remaining 2 cups milk and stir to combine. Transfer rice pudding to airtight container and refrigerate about 2 hours or until cold.

Blueberry Muffin Bread Pudding

The combination of vanilla and cinnamon with fresh blueberries gives this dessert extra richness. Challah bread also adds a nice natural sweetness. This bread pudding is BERRY delicious!

Serves:
10 to 12

Prep Time:
15 minutes

Pressure Cooking Time:
43 minutes

Release Method:
NATURAL

Ingredients:

1 ¼ cups whole milk

1 (14 oz.) can sweetened condensed milk

4 large eggs

2 teaspoons vanilla extract

2 teaspoons ground cinnamon

2 pints fresh blueberries

14 ounces challah bread, cut into 1-inch cubes

Directions:

1. Spray an 8-inch x 3-inch round cake pan with nonstick cooking spray.

2. In a large bowl, whisk milk, condensed milk, eggs, vanilla, and cinnamon until combined. Add blueberries and cubed bread to egg mixture and toss until bread has absorbed all of liquid.

3. Transfer bread pudding mixture to prepared pan. Tightly cover top of pan completely with lightly greased aluminum foil. Place small rack in pot. Add 2 cups of water. Place cake pan on rack.

4. Close and lock lid. Adjust pressure valve on top to AIRTIGHT, set COOKING TIME to 23 minutes, and press START.

5. When cooking cycle has finished, let pressure drop NATURALLY. Once all of pressure has released, turn lid, unlock, and open.

6. Remove pan from inner pot. Serve warm or let cool completely.

TIP You can substitute an equal amount of any other berry for the blueberries.

Serves:
10 to 12

Prep Time:
15 minutes

Pressure Cooking Time:
47 minutes (includes pressure release time)

Release Method:
NATURAL

Chocolate-Covered Raisin Bread Pudding

Chocolate-covered raisins are not just a movie snack any more! This ultra-chocolate-y bread pudding, with chocolate milk and chocolate covered raisins, is an amazing dessert!

Ingredients:

2 cups chocolate milk

2 tablespoons unsalted butter, melted

2 teaspoons vanilla extract

4 large eggs

2/3 cup sugar

14 ounces challah bread, cut into 1-inch cubes

1 cup dark chocolate covered raisins

Directions:

1. Spray 8-inch x 3-inch round cake pan with nonstick cooking spray.

2. In a large bowl, whisk chocolate milk, butter, vanilla, eggs, and sugar until combined.

3. Add cubed bread to egg mixture and toss until bread has absorbed all of liquid. Add chocolate covered raisins and mix gently until incorporated.

4. Transfer bread pudding mixture to prepared pan. Tightly cover top of pan completely with lightly greased aluminum foil. Place small rack in pot. Add 2 cups of water. Place cake pan on rack.

5. Close and lock lid. Adjust pressure valve on top to AIRTIGHT, set COOKING TIME to 27 minutes, and press START.

6. When cooking cycle has finished, let pressure drop NATURALLY. Once all of pressure has released, turn lid, unlock, and open. Remove pan from pot and serve warm.

TIP You can substitute any chocolate-covered dried fruit such as blueberries, pomegranate seeds, or cherries for the raisins.

Bananas Foster Bread Pudding

Soaking the bread cubes for a full hour in the flavorful egg and milk batter makes this dessert the ultimate in decadence. Top with vanilla ice cream or a caramel drizzle.

Serves:
10 to 12

Prep Time:
1 hour,
15 minutes

Pressure Cooking Time:
50 minutes
(including pressure release time)

Release Method:
NATURAL

Ingredients:

2 ½ cups milk

⅓ cup heavy cream

4 tablespoons unsalted butter, melted

2 teaspoons vanilla extract

1 tablespoon banana liqueur

4 tablespoons dark rum

5 large eggs

1 ½ teaspoons ground cinnamon

¾ cup sugar

18 ounces French baguette, cut into 2-inch cubes

3 bananas, sliced

Caramel sauce for garnish

Directions:

1. Spray 8-inch x 3-inch round cake pan with nonstick cooking spray.

2. In a large bowl, whisk milk, heavy cream, butter, vanilla, banana liqueur, rum, eggs, cinnamon, and sugar until evenly combined.

3. Add cubed bread to egg mixture and toss until completely coated. Cover bowl with plastic wrap and let sit for 30 minutes. Unwrap and toss bread mixture again. Wrap and let sit for another 30 minutes or until bread has absorbed most of liquid. Add sliced bananas and mix gently until incorporated.

4. Transfer bread pudding mixture to prepared pan. Tightly cover top of pan with lightly greased aluminum foil. Place small rack in pot. Add 2 cups of water. Place cake pan on rack.

5. Close and lock lid. Adjust pressure valve on top to AIRTIGHT, set COOKING TIME to 30 minutes, and press START.

6. When cooking cycle has finished, let pressure drop NATURALLY. Once all of pressure has released, turn lid, unlock, and open. Remove pan from pot and remove foil. Serve warm, drizzled with caramel sauce.

TIP For bananas foster a la mode, pair with your favorite ice cream.

Baked Apples

The combination of apples with oats, pecans, raisins, and "sugar and spice" makes this the perfect dessert on a cold, wintry day. Add the caramel drizzle for extra indulgence.

Serves:
4

Prep Time:
20 minutes

Pressure Cooking Time:
20 minutes

Release Method:
QUICK

Ingredients:

4 large Honey Crisp apples

2 teaspoons lemon juice

½ cup light brown sugar

⅓ cup quick one-minute oats

¾ teaspoon ground cinnamon

2 tablespoons unsalted butter, melted

⅓ cup chopped pecans

⅓ cup golden raisins

Caramel sauce for topping

Directions:

1. Remove core of apples, cutting within a half-inch of bottom of apple. Using a melon baller or small spoon, scoop a hole about 2-inches wide in each apple. Sprinkle each with ½ teaspoon lemon juice.

2. Place each apple on a piece of aluminum foil large enough to completely wrap apple. Set aside.

3. In a medium bowl, stir brown sugar, oats, and cinnamon until combined. Add melted butter, chopped pecans, and golden raisins and stir to combine. Divide mixture evenly between apples and stuff completely.

4. Wrap foil around each apple pinching firmly together at top. Place small rack into inner pot. Add 1 cup of water. Place wrapped apples on rack.

5. Close and lock lid. Adjust pressure valve on top to AIRTIGHT, set COOKING TIME to 20 minutes, and press START.

6. When cooking cycle has finished, release pressure by carefully setting valve to EXHAUST on top of lid. Once all of pressure has released, turn lid, unlock, and open.

7. Remove apples from inner pot, unwrap, and place on serving dish. Drizzle with caramel sauce before serving.

TIP Although this recipe calls for Honey Crisp apples, any sweet and firm apple such as Cortland, Empire, or McIntosh will work.

Makes:
1½ quarts

Prep Time:
20 minutes

**Pressure
Cooking Time:**
1 hour,
55 minutes
(includes
pressure
release time)

Release Method:
NATURAL
& QUICK

Apple Butter

There is nothing like warm, homemade apple butter to enhance any meal, or simply spread on a piece of toast as a great snack. The perfect amount of spice and vanilla provides deep flavor. Experiment with your favorite apples for new subtle flavors.

Ingredients:

2 ½ pounds Granny Smith apples, peeled, cored, and cut into 1-inch pieces

2 ½ pounds (any variety) red apples, peeled, cored, and cut into 1-inch pieces

1 cup light brown sugar

1 cup sugar

3 tablespoons lemon juice

1 tablespoon ground cinnamon

1 tablespoon vanilla extract

½ teaspoon ground allspice

¼ teaspoon salt

⅓ cup unsweetened apple juice

Directions:

1. Add all ingredients, in the order listed, to inner pot and stir to combine. Close and lock lid. Adjust pressure valve on top to AIRTIGHT, set COOKING TIME to 60 minutes, and press START.

2. When cooking cycle has finished, let pressure drop NATURALLY. Once all of pressure has released, turn lid, unlock, and open.

3. Puree cooked apples using a hand blender. Stir mixture until combined.

4. Close and lock lid. Adjust pressure valve on top to AIRTIGHT, set COOKING TIME to 35 minutes, and press START.

5. When cooking cycle has finished, release pressure by carefully setting valve to EXHAUST on top of lid. Once all of pressure has released, turn lid, unlock, and open.

6. Transfer mixture to airtight container and refrigerate 2 hours or until cold. Apple butter can be refrigerated for up to 1 month.

TIP Get creative and vary the flavor by adding more lemon, aged red wine, or balsamic vinegar.

CANNING

Strawberry Rhubarb Jam

Makes:
4 pints

Prep Time:
30 minutes

Pressure
Cooking Time:
10 minutes

Release Method:
QUICK

Canning Method:
BOILING
WATER BATH

Strawberries and rhubarb are nature's perfect combination of sweet and sour flavors in pies, sauces, and jams. This fresh jam recipe can be made in less than an hour! Rhubarb is available year round in the frozen food sections of many supermarkets. You can make a chunky version by processing the rhubarb for a shorter time before cooking.

Ingredients:

1 pound rhubarb, washed and chopped

3 pounds strawberries, hulled, cut in half

6 tablespoons dry pectin

¼ cup lemon juice

4 cups sugar

Directions:

1. Working in batches, puree rhubarb and strawberries in food processor until smooth.

2. Sterilize 4 (1 pint) canning jars and lids in boiling water for at least 10 minutes.

3. In a large pot, bring rhubarb, strawberries, pectin, and lemon juice to a boil. Add sugar and boil, stirring constantly, for 2 more minutes.

4. Ladle hot strawberry mixture into clean, hot jars leaving 1-inch headspace. Remove any air bubbles or foam on top. Clean rim, then seal jars.

5. Place short wire rack into inner pot. Place filled, sealed jars on rack. Pour hot water into pot until water level covers jars.

6. Close and lock lid. Adjust pressure valve on top to AIRTIGHT, press CANNING/PRESERVING button once and then continuously to increase time to 10 minutes, press START.

7. When cooking cycle has finished, release pressure by carefully setting valve to EXHAUST on top of lid. Once all of pressure has released, turn lid, unlock, and open.

8. Carefully remove jars and transfer to a towel or cooling rack. Cool completely. CAUTION: JARS ARE HOT.

9. Refrigerate after opening.

Peaches

Makes:
4 pints

Prep Time:
30 minutes

Pressure Cooking Time:
15 minutes

Release Method:
QUICK

Canning Method:
PRESSURE CANNING

Home-canned peaches have a wonderful texture and taste. Use the freshest and ripest fruit the to get the best quality. Once you compare these peaches to rubbery canned peaches, immersed in corn syrup, you will never go back.

Ingredients:

3 pounds fresh peaches

1 cup water

2 cups sugar

Directions:

1. Fill a large pot with water and bring to a boil. Fill a large bowl with cold water. Dip peaches in boiling water for 30 to 60 seconds then transfer to cold water. Peel skins, remove pit, and slice.

2. Sterilize 4 (1 pint) canning jars and lids in boiling water for at least 10 minutes.

3. In a medium pot, bring water and sugar to a boil and boil until sugar dissolves, about 5 minutes.

4. Place peaches into clean, hot jars. Ladle hot water into jars leaving 1-inch headspace. Remove any air bubbles. Clean rim, then seal jars.

5. Place short wire rack into inner pot. Place filled, sealed jars on rack. Pour hot water into pot until water level reaches ¼ of the way up sides of jars.

6. Close and lock lid. Adjust pressure valve on top to AIRTIGHT, press CANNING/PRESERVING button once and then continuously to increase time to 15 minutes, press START.

7. When cooking cycle has finished, release pressure by carefully setting valve to EXHAUST on top of lid. Once all of pressure has released, turn lid, unlock, and open.

8. Carefully remove jars and transfer to a towel or cooling rack. Cool completely. CAUTION: JARS ARE HOT

9. Refrigerate after opening.

Makes:
4 pints

Prep Time:
30 minutes

Pressure Cooking Time:
10 minutes

Release Method:
QUICK

Canning Method:
BOILING WATER BATH

Peach Jam

Just four ingredients can turn peaches into a delicious taste of summer all year round. Once you see how simple it is to make, you will want to make a batch every time there is a sale on fresh fruit at the market.

Ingredients:

16 fresh peaches, or about 4 pounds

3 tablespoons lemon juice

3 tablespoons dry pectin

3 cups sugar

Directions:

1. Fill a large pot with water and bring to a boil. Fill a large bowl with cold water. Dip tomatoes in boiling water for 30 to 60 seconds then transfer to cold water. Peel skins and remove pit. Working in batches, puree peaches in food processor until smooth.

2. Sterilize 4 (1 pint) canning jars and lids in boiling water for at least 10 minutes.

3. In a large pot, bring peach puree, lemon juice and pectin to a boil. Add sugar and boil, stirring constantly, for 2 minutes.

4. Ladle hot mixture into clean, hot jars leaving 1-inch headspace. Remove any air bubbles or foam on top. Clean rim, then seal jars.

5. Place short wire rack into inner pot. Place filled, sealed jars on rack. Pour hot water into pot until water level covers jars.

6. Close and lock lid. Adjust pressure valve on top to AIRTIGHT, press CANNING/ PRESERVING button once and then continuously to increase time to 10 minutes, press START.

7. When cooking cycle has finished, release pressure by carefully setting valve to EXHAUST on top of lid. Once all of pressure has released, turn lid, unlock, and open.

8. Carefully remove jars and transfer to a towel or cooling rack. Cool completely. CAUTION: JARS ARE HOT

9. Refrigerate after opening.

TIP **Want to make jam in January? You can substitute frozen peaches, but make sure you thaw and drain them prior to use.**

Applesauce

Makes:
4 pints

Prep Time:
45 minutes

Pressure Cooking Time:
20 minutes

Release Method:
QUICK

Canning Method:
PRESSURE CANNING

Applesauce is a must-have addition to your pantry. It is an instant side dish, especially with pork and chicken. Substitute applesauce for the oil in brownies, zucchini bread, and any quick bread recipes to reduce calories. It's also a great topper for oatmeal or yogurt.

Ingredients:

6 pounds apples, peeled, cored, and quartered

1 cup sugar

2 tablespoons lemon juice

Directions:

1. Sterilize 4 (1 pint) canning jars and lids in boiling water for at least 10 minutes.

2. In a large pot, covered, bring apples and 1 ½ cups water to a boil. Reduce heat to medium low. Cook apples until tender, stirring occasionally, about 15 minutes. Remove from heat and cool for 10 minutes.

3. Working in batches, puree apples in a food processor until smooth. Return apples to pot and add sugar and lemon juice. Bring to a low boil and cook until sugar dissolves, about 10 minutes.

4. Ladle hot applesauce into clean, hot jars leaving 1-inch headspace. Remove any air bubbles. Clean rim, then seal jars.

5. Place short wire rack into inner pot. Place filled, sealed jars on rack. Pour hot water into pot until water level reaches ¼ of the way up sides of jars.

6. Close and lock lid. Adjust pressure valve on top to AIRTIGHT, press CANNING/PRESERVING button once and then continuously to increase time to 20 minutes, press START.

7. When cooking cycle has finished, release pressure by carefully setting valve to EXHAUST on top of lid. Once all of pressure has released, turn lid, unlock, and open.

8. Carefully remove jars and transfer to a towel or cooling rack. Cool completely. CAUTION: JARS ARE HOT

9. Refrigerate after opening.

TIP You can make a chunky version by simply cutting the apples into ¾-inch pieces.

Mild Tomato Salsa

Makes:
4 pints

Prep Time:
30 minutes

Pressure
Cooking Time:
10 minutes

Release Method:
QUICK

Canning Method:
BOILING
WATER BATH

Next to ketchup, tomato salsa is probably the most popular condiment around the world. There are many wonderful salsa recipes. Use your pressure cooker to can your first batch using this basic mild recipe. When you see how easy it is, try a few additional recipes. How about spicy, hot, mango or blueberry? Build your own salsa pantry collection and you can add a salsa bar to any taco night or big game party.

Ingredients:

20 tomatoes

2 medium onions, diced

1 green bell pepper, seeded and diced

2 jalapeno peppers, seeded and diced

½ cup lime juice

3 cloves garlic, minced

2 teaspoons ground cumin

1 tablespoon salt

1 tablespoon ground black pepper

1 cup chopped fresh cilantro

Directions:

1. Fill a large pot with water and bring to a boil. Fill a large bowl with cold water. Dip tomatoes in boiling water for 30 to 60 seconds then transfer to cold water. Peel skins, remove seeds, and chop half of tomatoes. Working in batches, puree remaining half of tomatoes in food processor until smooth.

2. Sterilize 4 (1 pint) canning jars and lids in boiling water for at least 10 minutes.

3. In a large pot, combine the chopped tomatoes with the pureed tomatoes. Add onions, peppers, lime juice, garlic, cumin, salt, black pepper, and cilantro and stir to combine. Bring to a boil.

4. Place salsa mixture into clean, hot jars. Remove any air bubbles. Clean rim, then seal jars.

5. Place short wire rack into inner pot. Place filled, sealed jars on rack. Pour hot water into pot until water level covers jars.

6. Close and lock lid. Adjust pressure valve on top to AIRTIGHT, press CANNING/PRESERVING button once and then continuously to increase time to 10 minutes, press START.

7. When cooking cycle has finished, release pressure by carefully setting valve to EXHAUST on e top of lid. Once all of pressure has released, turn lid, unlock, and open.

8. Carefully remove jars and transfer to a towel or cooling rack. Cool completely. CAUTION: JARS ARE HOT

9. Refrigerate after opening.

Makes:
4 pints

Prep Time:
45 minutes

Pressure Cooking Time:
20 minutes

Release Method:
QUICK

Canning Method:
PRESSURE CANNING

Spaghetti Sauce

Homemade spaghetti sauce is a must-have in every pantry. Commercially-canned sauces tend to have too much salt and other undesirable chemicals. When you make this recipe, you will feel good knowing all the fresh ingredients that you are including.

Ingredients:

6 pounds tomatoes

2 tablespoons olive oil

1 medium onion, chopped

4 cloves garlic, minced

3 tablespoons Italian seasoning, we recommend Great Flavors® Italian Seasoning

2 tablespoons sugar

1 teaspoon salt

1 teaspoon ground black pepper

Directions:

1. Fill a large pot with water and bring to a boil. Fill a large bowl with cold water. Dip tomatoes in boiling water for 30 to 60 seconds then transfer to cold water. Peel skins, remove seeds, and chop.

2. Sterilize 4 (1 pint) canning jars and lids in boiling water for at least 10 minutes.

3. In a large pot, bring tomatoes, oil, onion, garlic, Italian seasoning, sugar, salt, and pepper to a boil. Reduce heat to medium low. Cook, stirring occasionally, until tomatoes are tender, about 15 minutes. Remove from heat and cool for 10 minutes.

4. Working in batches, puree tomato mixture in food processor until smooth. Return to pot and bring to a boil.

5. Ladle hot tomato mixture into clean, hot jars leaving 1-inch headspace. Remove any air bubbles. Clean rim, then seal jars.

6. Place short wire rack into inner pot. Place filled, sealed jars on rack. Pour hot water into pot until water level reaches ¼ of the way up sides of jars.

7. Close and lock lid. Adjust pressure valve on top to AIRTIGHT, press CANNING/ PRESERVING button once and then continuously to increase time to 20 minutes, press START.

8. When cooking cycle has finished, release pressure by carefully setting valve to EXHAUST on top of lid. Once all of pressure has released, turn lid, unlock, and open.

9. Carefully remove jars and transfer to a towel or cooling rack. Cool completely. CAUTION: JARS ARE HOT. Refrigerate after opening.

 Green Beans

If you count tomatoes as a fruit, then more green beans are home canned than any other vegetable in America. When home gardeners are flooded with more summer green beans than they can possible eat, pressure canning is a great way preserve this fresh-picked produce. Put them away in your pantry and have them on hand to add to soups and casseroles or use as a side dish to any meal.

Makes:
4 pints

Prep Time:
30 minutes

Pressure Cooking Time:
15 minutes

Release Method:
QUICK

Canning Method:
PRESSURE CANNING

Ingredients:

4 cups water

1 ¾ pounds green beans, ends trimmed to fit into jars

2 teaspoons salt, divided

Directions:

1. Sterilize 4 (1 pint) canning jars and lids in boiling water for at least 10 minutes.

2. In a medium pot bring water to a boil.

3. Place green beans and ½ teaspoon salt into clean, hot jars. Ladle hot water into jars leaving 1-inch headspace. Remove any air bubbles. Clean rim, then seal jars.

4. Place short wire rack into inner pot. Place filled sealed jars on rack. Pour hot water into pot until water level reaches ¼ of the way up sides of jars.

5. Close and lock lid. Adjust pressure valve on top to AIRTIGHT, press the CANNING/PRESERVING button once and then continuously to increase time to 15 minutes, press START.

6. When cooking cycle has finished, release pressure by carefully setting valve to EXHAUST on top of lid. Once all of pressure has released, turn lid, unlock, and open.

7. Carefully remove jars and transfer to a towel or cooling rack. Cool completely. CAUTION: JARS ARE HOT

8. Refrigerate after opening.

Makes:
4 pints

Prep Time:
35 minutes

Pressure Cooking Time:
7 minutes

Release Method:
QUICK

Canning Method:
BOILING WATER BATH

Giardiniera Vegetables

Italian Giardiniera is also called "sotto aceti," which means "under vinegar." You will love this vegetable medley chopped and served as an antipasto or on bruschetta. You'll get huge raves by serving it in a pasta salad, mixed into green salads, or as a topping for burgers and hot dogs.

Ingredients:

2 ½ cups water

1 cup white vinegar

½ cup sugar

⅓ cup salt

1 tablespoon celery seeds

1 tablespoon mustard seeds

4 cloves garlic, minced

1 teaspoon dried oregano

2 cups cauliflower, cut into small florets

2 celery ribs, cut into 1-inch pieces

1 cup baby carrots

½ red bell pepper, cut into 1-inch pieces

½ medium onion, cut into 1-inch pieces

Directions:

1. Sterilize 4 (1 pint) canning jars and lids in boiling water for at least 10 minutes.

2. In a large pot, bring water, vinegar, sugar, salt, celery seed, mustard seed, garlic, and oregano to a boil. Boil for 5 minutes.

3. In a medium bowl, combine cauliflower, celery, carrots, pepper, and onion.

4. Place vegetables into clean, hot jars. Ladle hot liquid into jars leaving 1-inch headspace. Remove any air bubbles. Clean rim, then seal jars.

5. Place short wire rack into inner pot. Place filled, sealed jars on rack. Pour hot water into pot until water level covers jars.

6. Close and lock lid. Adjust pressure valve on top to AIRTIGHT, press the CANNING/PRESERVING button once and then continuously to increase time to 7 minutes, press START.

7. When cooking cycle has finished, release pressure by carefully setting valve to EXHAUST on top of lid. Once all of pressure has released, turn lid, unlock, and open.

8. Carefully remove jars and transfer to a towel or cooling rack. Cool completely. CAUTION: JARS ARE HOT

9. Refrigerate after opening.

Quick Dill Pickles

This quick dill pickle recipe couldn't be easier. If you haven't canned before, make this recipe and then try some variations, such as garlic, grape leaves, flavored or unusual vinegars, Kosher, and more. I like to make this same recipe in slices, wedges and chunks. Each has its special use for sides, on sandwiches, in salsas, etc.

Makes:
4 pints

Prep Time:
30 minutes

Pressure Cooking Time:
10 minutes

Release Method:
QUICK

Canning Method:
BOILING WATER BATH

Ingredients:

2 pounds pickling cucumbers

2 ¼ cups water

1 ¼ cups white vinegar

¾ cup sugar

⅓ cup salt

2 tablespoons pickling spice

½ cup minced fresh dill

4 cloves garlic, minced

Directions:

1. Sterilize 4 (1 pint) canning jars and lids in boiling water for at least 10 minutes.

2. Cut cucumbers in half and so that they fit into jars. In a large pot, bring water, vinegar, sugar, salt, and pickling spice to a boil. Boil for 5 minutes.

3. Place cucumbers into clean, hot jars. Add 2 tablespoons dill and 1 teaspoon minced garlic to each jar. Ladle hot liquid into jars leaving 1-inch headspace. Remove any air bubbles. Clean rim, then seal jars.

4. Place short wire rack into inner pot. Place filled, sealed jars on rack. Pour hot water into pot until water level covers jars.

5. Close and lock lid. Adjust pressure valve on top to AIRTIGHT, press CANNING/PRESERVING button once and then continuously to increase time to 10 minutes, press START.

6. When cooking cycle has finished, release pressure by carefully setting valve to EXHAUST on top of lid. Once all of pressure has released, turn lid, unlock, and open.

7. Carefully remove jars and transfer to a towel or cooling rack. Cool completely. CAUTION: JARS ARE HOT.

8. Refrigerate after opening.

Bread & Butter Pickles

Fresh bread and butter pickles are perfect as a staple to add to any favorite sandwich, or even as a snack with your cheese and crackers. The sweet and tangy flavors are particularly enhanced when you make them yourself.

Makes:
4 pints

Prep Time:
35 minutes

Pressure Cooking Time:
10 minutes

Release Method:
QUICK

Canning Method:
BOILING WATER BATH

Ingredients:

1 ½ **pounds pickling cucumbers**

2 **cups water**

1 **cup white vinegar**

1 ½ **cups sugar**

¼ **cup salt**

1 **tablespoon mustard seed**

1 **tablespoon celery seed**

1 **teaspoon ground turmeric**

2 **medium onions, sliced thin**

Directions:

1. Sterilize 4 (1 pint) canning jars and lids in boiling water for at least 10 minutes.

2. Cut cucumbers into 3/16-inch slices.

3. In a large pot, bring water, vinegar, sugar, salt, mustard seed, celery seed, and turmeric to boil. Boil for 5 minutes.

4. Place cucumbers and onions into clean, hot jars. Ladle hot liquid into jars leaving 1-inch headspace. Remove any air bubbles. Clean rim, then seal jars.

5. Place short wire rack into inner pot. Place filled sealed jars on rack. Pour hot water into pot until water level covers jars.

6. Close and lock lid. Adjust pressure valve on top to AIRTIGHT, press CANNING/PRESERVING button once and then continuously to increase time to 10 minutes, press START.

7. When cooking cycle has finished, release pressure by carefully setting valve to EXHAUST on top of lid. Once all of pressure has released, turn lid, unlock, and open.

8. Carefully remove jars and transfer to a towel or cooling rack. Cool completely. CAUTION: JARS ARE HOT

9. Refrigerate after opening.

TIP **Not every cucumber will work for pickles. Make sure to buy pickling cucumbers as other varieties are not firm enough to maintain crispness after pickling.**

POULTRY COOKING CHART

TYPE	SIZE	LIQUID	TIME	TEMP	RELEASE	FROZEN
Chicken, breast (bone in)	Any	½ cup	13 min.	High	Quick	Plus 8 min.
Chicken, breast (boneless)	Any	½ cup	10 min.	High	Quick	Plus 7 min.
Chicken, ground	Any	⅔ cup	4 min.	High	Quick	N/A
Chicken, leg quarters	2 lb.	1 cup	14 min.	High	Natural	Plus 10 min.
Chicken, thighs	2 lb.	⅔ cup	12 min.	High	Quick	Plus 8 min.
Chicken, whole	3–5 lb.	2 cups	30 min.	High	Natural	Plus 15 min.
Chicken, wings	4 lb.	⅔ cup	15 min.	High	Quick	N/A
Cornish Hen	2 hens	1 cup	12 min.	High	Quick	Plus 10 min.
Turkey, breast (bone-in)	3–5 lb.	2 cups	30 min.	High	Natural	Plus 15 min.
Turkey, breast (boneless)	2–3 lb.	1 cup	18–20 min.	High	Natural	Plus 10 min.
Turkey, ground	Any	1 cup	4 min.	High	Quick	N/A
Turkey Legs	2–4 legs	1 ½ cups	18–20 min.	High	Natural	Plus 10–12 min.

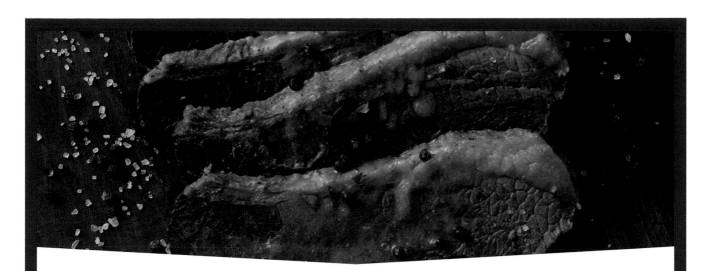

BEEF COOKING CHART

TYPE	SIZE	LIQUID	TIME	TEMP	RELEASE	FROZEN
Brisket	2–3 lb.	Covered	65 min.	High	Natural	N/A
Brisket	4–5 lb.	Covered	80 min.	High	Natural	N/A
Chuck Roast	3–4 lb.	2 cups	70 min.	High	Natural	N/A
Corned Beef	2–3 lb.	Covered	60 min.	High	Natural	N/A
Corned Beef	4–5 lb.	Covered	80 min.	High	Natural	N/A
Flank Steak	2–3 lb.	1 cup	22 min.	High	Natural	Plus 8 min.
Ground Beef	1–2 lb.	⅔ cup	5 min.	High	Quick	N/A
Oxtails	Any	Covered	45 min.	High	Natural	N/A
Rib Roast	3–4 lb.	2 cups	60 min.	High	Natural	N/A
Round Roast	3–4 lb.	2 cups	70 min.	High	Natural	N/A
Shanks	Any	1 ½ cups	38 min.	High	Natural	N/A
Short Ribs	Any	2 cups	25 min.	High	Natural	Plus 10 min.
Shoulder Roast	3–4 lb.	2 cups	70 min.	High	Natural	N/A
Steak	1-inch thick	⅔ cup	16 min.	High	Quick	Plus 5 min.
Stew Meat	1-inch cubes	1 cup	18 min.	High	Natural	Plus 8 min.

PORK & LAMB COOKING CHART

TYPE	SIZE	LIQUID	TIME	TEMP	RELEASE	FROZEN
Ham, hock	Any	Covered	45 min.	High	Natural	N/A
Ham, steak	2–4 steaks	½ cup	6 min.	High	Quick	Plus 5 min.
Ham, whole	3–5 lb.	3 cups	40 min.	High	Natural	Plus 25 min.
Lamb, chop	½ inch	½ cup	6 min.	High	Quick	Plus 7 min.
Lamb, chop	1 inch	½ cup	10 min.	High	Quick	Plus 10 min.
Lamb, leg	5–7 lb.	2 cups	50 min.	High	Natural	Plus 20 min.
Lamb, shank	Any	1 ½ cups	30 min.	High	Natural	Plus 10 min.
Pork, chops	½ inch	½ cup	8 min.	High	Quick	Plus 7 min.
Pork, chops	1 inch	½ cup	12 min.	High	Quick	Plus 10 min.
Pork, roast	3–5 lb.	2 cups	80 min.	High	Natural	N/A
Pork, roast (2-inch slice)	3–5 lb.	2 cups	45 min.	High	Natural	N/A
Pork, baby back ribs	1 rack	1 cup	18 min.	High	Natural	N/A
Pork, spareribs	2–4 lb.	1 cup	20 min.	High	Natural	N/A
Pork, tenderloin	1–2 lb.	⅓ cup	15 min.	High	Natural	N/A
Sausage	Any	Covered	8 min.	High	Quick	Plus 7 min.

SEAFOOD COOKING CHART

TYPE	SIZE	LIQUID	TIME	TEMP	RELEASE	FROZEN
Clams	Any	½ cup	5 min.	High	Quick	N/A
Cod	Two 4-oz. filets	½ cup	4 min.	High	Quick	Plus 4 min.
Crab Legs	Small	½ cup	3 min.	High	Quick	N/A
Lobster Tail	½ pound	½ cup	4 min.	High	Quick	Plus 4 min.
Mussels	Any	½ cup	3 min.	High	Quick	N/A
Salmon	Two 4-oz. filets	½ cup	5 min.	High	Quick	Plus 5 min.
Scallops, bay	Any	½ cup	1 min.	High	Quick	Plus 2 min.
Shrimp	Medium	½ cup	2 min.	High	Quick	Plus 1 min.
Shrimp	Jumbo	½ cup	3 min.	High	Quick	Plus 2 min.
Tilapia	Two 4-oz. filets	½ cup	2 min.	High	Quick	Plus 4 min.
Tuna	Two 4-oz. filets	½ cup	4 min.	High	Quick	Plus 5 min.

VEGETABLES COOKING CHART

TYPE	SIZE	LIQUID	TIME	TEMP	RELEASE	FROZEN
Artichokes	Whole	1 cup	10 min.	High	Quick	N/A
Asparagus	Thick	½ cup	2 min.	High	Quick	N/A
Beets	1-inch pieces	¾ cup	10 min.	High	Quick	N/A
Beets	Whole	¾ cup	20 min.	High	Quick	N/A
Brussels Sprouts	Whole	½ cup	4 min.	High	Quick	N/A
Butternut Squash	1-inch pieces	1 cup	5 min.	High	Quick	N/A
Cabbage	Quartered	Covered	4 min.	High	Quick	N/A
Carrots	1-inch pieces	½ cup	4 min.	High	Quick	N/A
Corn, on cob	Any	1 cup	3 min.	High	Quick	N/A
Eggplant	1-inch pieces	½ cup	3 min.	High	Quick	N/A
Green Beans	Any	½ cup	3 min.	High	Quick	N/A
Potatoes, New	Whole	1 cup	4 min.	High	Quick	N/A
Potatoes, Russet	1-inch pieces	1 cup	9 min.	High	Quick	N/A
Potatoes, Sweet	Whole	1 cup	17 min.	High	Quick	N/A
Rutabaga	1-inch pieces	1 cup	5 min.	High	Quick	N/A
Acorn Squash	Halved	1 cup	7 min.	High	Quick	N/A
Squash, Yellow	1-inch pieces	½ cup	2 min.	High	Quick	N/A
Turnip	1-inch pieces	½ cup	4 min.	High	Quick	N/A
Zucchini	1-inch pieces	½ cup	2 min.	High	Quick	N/A

PASTA & GRAINS COOKING CHART

TYPE	SIZE	LIQUID	TIME	TEMP	RELEASE	FROZEN
Barley	1 cup	4 cups	18 min.	High	Natural	N/A
Couscous	1 cup	1 ½ cups	3 min.	High	Quick	N/A
Pasta, bow tie	1 cup	3 cups	9 min.	High	Quick	N/A
Pasta, elbow macaroni	1 cup	3 cups	12 min.	High	Quick	N/A
Pasta, orzo	1 cup	3 ½ cups	4 min.	High	Quick	N/A
Pasta, shell	1 cup	3 cups	12 min.	High	Quick	N/A
Pasta, tortellini (dried)	1 cup	3 cups	5 min.	High	Quick	N/A
Pasta, ziti	1 cup	3 cups	13 min.	High	Quick	N/A
Quinoa	1 cup	2 cups	6 min.	High	Natural	N/A
Rice, brown (short grain)	1 cup	2 cups	7 min.	High	Natural	N/A
Rice, brown (medium grain)	1 cup	2 cups	6 min.	High	Natural	N/A
Rice, brown (long grain)	1 cup	2 cups	5 min.	High	Natural	N/A
Rice. white (short grain)	1 cup	2 ½ cups	5 min.	High	Natural	N/A
Rice, white (medium grain)	1 cup	2 cups	4 min.	High	Natural	N/A
Rice, white (long grain)	1 cup	1 ¾ cups	7 min.	High	Natural	N/A
Wheat Berries	1 cup	3 cups	30 min.	High	Natural	N/A

BEANS & LEGUMES COOKING CHART

TYPE	SIZE	LIQUID	TIME	TEMP	RELEASE	FROZEN
Black Beans	Any	Covered	20 min.	High	Natural	N/A
Black-Eyed Peas	Any	Covered	12 min.	High	Natural	N/A
Cannellini	Any	Covered	35 min.	High	Natural	N/A
Fava	Any	Covered	40 min.	High	Natural	N/A
Garbanzo (Chick Peas)	Any	Covered	35 min.	High	Natural	N/A
Great Northern	Any	Covered	28 min.	High	Natural	N/A
Kidney	Any	Covered	22 min.	High	Natural	N/A
Lentils	Any	Covered	15 min.	High	Natural	N/A
Lima	Any	Covered	14 min.	High	Natural	N/A
Navy	Any	Covered	20 min.	High	Natural	N/A
Peanuts, raw	Any	Covered	75 min.	High	Natural	N/A
Pinto	Any	Covered	24 min.	High	Natural	N/A

PRESSURE COOKER SIZE CONVERSION CHART

How to Adjust Our Recipes if Your Pressure Cooker Has a Different Pressure Output

The recipes in this book were written and tested using an Elite 8-quart Pressure Cooker, which is set at 12 psi., or pounds per square inch. However, our recipes can be prepared using any digital or stovetop pressure cooker. Some cookers display the cooking pressure as "HIGH" or "LOW," while others display them in psi. So how does this effect cooking? For example, if your pressure cooker has a high setting of 15 psi., the total pressure cooking time of our recipes should be reduced by approximately 15%. Before using any pressure cooker for the first time, it is highly recommended that you read your cooker's manual from front to back to fully understand how to safely and correctly operate it.

	10 QUART plus 25%	8 QUART Standard	6 QUART Less 33%	4 QUART Less 66%
Pounds	2 ½ lbs	2 lb.	1 lb.	⅔ lb.
Cups	2 ½ lbs	2 cups	1⅓ cups	⅔ cup
Ounces	2 ½ oz.	2 oz.	1⅓ cups	⅔ oz.
Tablespoons	1 tbsp. plus	1 tbsp.	2 tsp.	1 tsp.
Teaspoons	1⅓ tsp.	1 tsp.	⅔ tsp.	⅓ tsp.
Whole or Slice	1¼ whole	1 whole	⅔ whole	⅓ whole

PANTRY LIST

SPICE RACK

All-Purpose Seasoning

Almond Extract

Baking Powder

Baking Soda

Cajun Seasoning

Cinnamon, ground

Cloves, ground

Coriander, ground

Cumin, ground

Curry Powder

Fajita Seasoning

Garlic Pepper

Garlic Powder

Ginger, ground

Italian Seasoning

Mustard, ground

Onion Powder

Oregano

Paprika, smoked

Pepper, ground black

Pepper flakes, crushed red

Salt, table

Sugar, granulated and brown

Thyme

Vanilla Extract

PANTRY BASICS

Barbecue Sauce

Barley

Beans, dried

Bread Crumbs

Brown Rice

Buffalo Wing Sauce

Fruit, dried

Hoisin Sauce

Maple Syrup

Nuts

Pasta, dried

Pasta Sauce (Marinara, Vodka, and Alfredo)

Pineapple slices, canned

Raisins

Red Wine

Soy Sauce

Stock (Chicken, Beef, and Vegetable)

Sweetened Condensed Milk

Tomatoes, crusted, diced, paste, and sauce

Vinegars

REFRIGERATOR

Apple Cider

Cheeses

Cream, light

Cream cheese

Ginger, fresh

Mustard, Dijon

Onions CR: Would omit this

Orange Juice

Pesto, basil

FREEZER

Chicken Breasts, uncooked whole and grilled strips

Cranberries

Meatballs, cocktail and entrée sized

Pork Chops

Puff Pastry

Ravioli

INDEX

INDEX

INDEX

INDEX

GREAT FLAVORS®

Using Great Flavors® Concentrates and Spices

A key principle of culinary success and delectable meal making, especially pressure-cooking, is that you should grab every opportunity to add scrumptious flavor. That's why nearly all of the recipes in this book use stocks or broths instead of water. While creating your own stock can be satisfying it's also incredibly time consuming and purchasing pre-made stock or broth becomes quite costly. Plus, most bouillon cubes or liquid stock are high in sodium and only a portion of the liquid stock in its cartons is even needed, wasting much of it. We recommend Great Flavors® concentrates and spices to give you the most savory options resulting in the most tasty meals.

We strongly suggest using the 4 flavors of meat and vegetable Great Flavors® concentrates to enhance the recipes in this book. The Great Flavors® concentrates are slow simmered and reduced to a paste for easy measuring, plus by adding water it creates delicious instant stocks and soups. Each squeezable jar makes 72 cups which is equal to 18 cartons of liquid stock.

Unlike liquid stock, Great Flavors® concentrates do not have to be refrigerated even after opening. Plus the exciting health news is that they are reduced sodium, gluten free and have no added MSG.

Another wonderful benefit to Great Flavors® concentrates is they can eliminate the prep-step of browning in pressure and slow cooking recipes that call for this in advance. You simply add a tablespoon of the appropriate Great Flavors® Concentrate for an instant boost of the outstanding flavor that browning gives to any meat recipe. While none of the recipes in this book require adding extra concentrate, many of the gravies and sauces in these recipes will have a more robust flavor when you add an extra teaspoon, or so to taste, before serving. We recommend having all flavors of Great Flavors® concentrates as a staple in your pantry to always have the option of taking your recipes to the next level, especially when pressure cooking. Also be sure to try Great Flavors® 6 spice blends, especially the All Purpose Seasoning in place of Salt and Pepper in most recipes.